PROPAGANDA TECHNIQUE
IN WORLD WAR I

M.I.T. STUDIES IN COMPARATIVE POLITICS

Under the general editorship of Harold D. Lasswell, Daniel Lerner, and Ithiel de Sola Pool.

The Emerging Elite: A Study of Political Leadership in Ceylon, Marshall R. Singer, 1964.

The Turkish Political Elite, Frederick W. Frey, 1965.

World Revolutionary Elites: Studies in Coercive Ideological Movements, Harold D. Lasswell and Daniel Lerner, editors, 1965.

Language of Politics: Studies in Quantitative Semantics, Harold D. Lasswell, Nathan Leites, and Associates, 1965 (reissue).

The General Inquirer: A Computer Approach to Content Analysis, Philip J. Stone, Dexter C. Dunphy, Marshall S. Smith, and Daniel M. Ogilvie, 1966.

Political Elites: A Select Computerized Bibliography, Carl Beck and J. Thomas McKechnie, 1968.

Force and Folly: Essays on Foreign Affairs and the History of Ideas, Hans Speier, 1969.

Quantitative Ecological Analysis in the Social Sciences, Mattei Dogan and Stein Rokkan, editors, 1969.

Euratlantica: Changing Perspectives of the European Elites, Daniel Lerner and Morton Gorden, 1969.

Revolution and Political Leadership: Algeria, 1954-1968, William B. Quandt, 1969.

The Prestige Press: A Comparative Study of Political Symbols, Ithiel de Sola Pool, 1970.

The Vanishing Peasant: Innovation and Change in French Agriculture, Henri Mendras, 1971.

Psychological Warfare against Nazi Germany: The Sykewar Campaign, D-Day to VE-Day, Daniel Lerner, 1971 (reissue).

Propaganda Technique in World War I, Harold D. Lasswell, 1971 (reissue).

Propaganda Technique

in

World War I

HAROLD D. LASSWELL

THE M.I.T. PRESS

Cambridge, Massachusetts, and London, England

Original edition published under the title *Propaganda Technique in the World War* in London in 1927 by Kegan Paul, Trench, Trubner & Co., Ltd. Introduction copyright © 1971 by The Massachusetts Institute of Technology

First M.I.T. Press paperback edition, February 1971

ISBN 0 262 12044 5 (hardcover)
ISBN 0 262 62018 9 (paperback)

Library of Congress Catalog Card Number: 77-148852

Printed in the United States of America

To my Parents
ANNA PRATHER LASSWELL
LINDEN DOWNEY LASSWELL

CONTENTS

INTRODUCTION*

HAROLD D. LASSWELL
JACKSON A. GIDDENS

I.

IN COMMON with so many doctoral dissertations this book is the modest spin-off of an initial plan so grand that obtaining a Ph.D. would have become a life work. The original project was to devise a theoretical scheme for the study of "international attitudes" and to survey the literature for plausible hypotheses and pertinent data. The scheme has never been executed in detail. It has, however, been an important topic-selector in subsequent research. For instance, the preliminary study of international attitudes directed attention to the individual and collective role of *intensity* levels, which remains a tantalizing domain in spite of later advances in the procedures designed to explore the "unconscious" or the role of "fundamental impulses" in personality, politics, and society.

Intensities are not satisfactorily disposed of by the use of metaphors, especially metaphors of the kind that are commonly extrapolated from physics. It is true that "mass-energy" equations are reliable tools for describing the "resource" component of a political process, so that the intensity of international conflict is measurable to the extent that intensity is defined as persistence against opposition. The

---

* Part 1 is chiefly the work of Harold D. Lasswell; Part 2 of Jackson A. Giddens.

resources mobilized in opposing coalitions can be described in terms of the number of combatants, the weight of supplies, and the per capita consumption of mechanical, electromagnetic, nuclear, and other varieties of physical power. However, the intensity dimension involves the predisposition to act, and is not only measurable by "resources mobilized." The "words" uttered in interview situations may be more adequate predictors of future conduct than the resources expended in a past conflict. Small numbers with inferior resources may outlast the enemy.

The choice of propaganda as a topic of study grew out of a wish to examine the place occupied by the symbolic among the nonsymbolic events of war or peace. If we regard subjective events as symbolic events, then the realms of overt "behavioral" and "resource" change are nonsymbolic events. The behavior involved in a sequence of communication is nonsymbolic in the sense that it is sign manipulation, and signs are physical events (namely, muscle movements, sounds, and the like). Nevertheless, signs are recognized to be particularly satisfactory indicators of moods and images; in a word, of the symbolic.

Our inferences about the symbolic are in no way restricted to the interpretation of signs, or the specialized physical events that serve as media of communication. When we look at the surviving signs on an ancient battlefield — the inscriptions — it may not be possible to read them. But from the nature and distribution of broken shields and lances and other artifacts it is not difficult to infer who perceived himself as mortally opposed to whom. It is evident that our task of exploring the outside world is both assisted and endangered by our "inside" observation. On reflection we discover our peculiar dependence on the inner symbol stream in evaluating hypotheses about symbol streams elsewhere in the environment.

The focus on propaganda "technique" was in some degree a reaction to a long period of preoccupation with the "contemplative" approach to international attitudes. The formal scheme that I was perfecting seemed to produce an endless list of potentially significant factors and a near-infinity of hypothetical interdependencies. Biological, psychological, and cultural variables proliferated with every serious probe into existing disciplines, and this was a moment when political scientists, especially at the University of Chicago, were aflame with interdisciplinary interests. The principal advantage of shifting to a "manipulative" approach was evident: it set limits to the inquiry by providing it with criteria.

War propaganda was a problem that kept one rooted in political science and at the same time marked off a single furrow in the immense field of "international attitudes." It was possible to submerge oneself in a definite body of empirical detail, and this carried with it an opportunity to think about the ways in which theoretical constructs could be fruitfully related to concrete circumstances. What categories of intermediate generality would bridge the enormous gap between the universal manifold of events so elegantly formalized by A. N. Whitehead, for example, and the legacy of political theory extending from Aristotle through Machiavelli and Hobbes to Marx, plus the sociopsychological-biological theories so prominent in contemporary times? The study of propaganda in World War I was not a "vacation from theory" but an exercise in the discovery of appropriate theory.

At that time my greatest interest was in inventing categories that, while hovering close to the "political" features of a situation, could be readily linked to the larger and smaller "psychological" and "cultural" components of the total field of interaction where political phenomena occur. Two principal questions arose in connection with technique: one was how to classify the "content" of propaganda; the second was how to summarize the "procedures" employed in organizing and executing propaganda operations.

Several other aspects of war propaganda are equally valid parts of the whole, notably the effect of propaganda considerations on policy and the impact of propaganda on collective attitudes. However, it was then out of the question to deal with either issue in detail. For example, the measurement of results was in its infancy and archives were closed.

Perhaps it should be made explicit that the use of the word "suggestion" in the text of *Propaganda Technique in the World War* is of little conceptual importance. It was selected solely because of its "subjective" connotations, and without regard to any particular theory of suggestion current in psychiatric, psychological, or social-psychological circles. The difficulty of the term "suggestion" is that it carries a superfluous and ambiguous connotation regarding the "intention" of the communicator and the "responsiveness" of the audience. In later publications I dropped it as terms from communication theory became more acceptable (e.g., symbol, sign, message) and as the distinction between *availability for* attention and the *orientation of* attention became clearer.

However, the fact that my work was not attached to any well-developed theory of suggestion should not imply that I was not in possession of, or was uninfluenced by, comprehensive psychocultural theories. On the contrary, my analysis of international attitudes (partially incorporated in such later publications as *World Politics and Personal Insecurity* and *Power and Society*) had produced a preliminary theoretical system. However, I adopted the tactic of leaving the system latent as a means of widening my experience of the concrete configurations of politics. I allowed fundamental distinctions to stay in the background while I set up and explored categories of lesser generality, more tightly bound to particular contexts of time and place.

The background distinctions referred to "perspectives" of identity, value demand, and expectation, as well as to "operations" in the realm of behavioral and resource impact. Stimulated by George Herbert Mead's analysis of the self, it seemed important to emphasize the identity of the propagandist and his audience. A convenient breakdown distinguished four principal groups of participants who were referred to, or directly addressed, by the spokesmen of every nation-state: "our" domestic audience; "our enemy," "our (or their) allies," and "neutrals."

The classification of a particular propaganda statement or flow of statements went beyond a consideration of symbols of identity to the mode of presenting symbols of the self or other in a favorable or unfavorable light. As later standardized, a symbol was said to be "indulged" or "deprived" in terms of a general "value." The value categories were not explicitly listed in *Propaganda Technique*, nor was the distinction expressly drawn between "values" (such as "power" or "respect") and "institutions" (such as the specialized "perspectives" and "operations" employed in the shaping and sharing of a given set of values). Corresponding distinctions were, however, part of the original outline of international attitudes, because much of my course work had been in economics, and I was aware of the fruitful tension between classical "value" theorists and "institutionalists" in economics. I was, however, as yet unwilling to commit myself to a comprehensive formal system in which the shaping and sharing of wealth would be put in the context of power, respect, and other value-institution sectors of society. It is accurate to say that *Propaganda Technique* is an effort to allow the phenomena to speak for themselves and to influence the form eventually taken by the conceptual model to be explicated.

Reference has been made to the theory of self that lay behind the propagandist-audience analysis. Another background distinction was between "value demands" and "expectations," the latter term alluding to matter-of-fact references to past, present, or future events. "The illusion of victory," for instance, deals chiefly with expectations. "War aims," "guilt," and "satanism" are "value demands." The last two have ethical or religious connotations and include much of what was later called "rectitude" or the demand for responsible conduct.

My study of war propaganda was as much concerned with the *procedures* of propaganda as with the discovery of useful categories of content analysis. The seminal argument developed in connection with procedures emphasized the overwhelming significance of operating within the framework of current predispositions. Propaganda was often talked about as though it were a magical force emancipated from the limitations of time, place, and figure. *Propaganda Technique* emphatically rejected such a view, and the rejection is well founded. We know that propagandists are socialized in bodies politic whose specific contextual features set limits on potential perception, imagination, and behavior and that propagandists seek to influence audiences whose socialization is similarly circumscribed. At best the propagandist is selective. He discerns a potential reservoir of discontent or aspiration and searches for ways of discharging the discontent and harnessing the aspirations so that they harmonize with his policy objectives. The available means of mobilizing collective action depend, in turn, on words and word equivalents whose signification is already circumscribed by the predispositional patterns present in the political arena. Furthermore, the existing predispositional patterns themselves set limits on what can be done. These patterns include *value structures* (who is elite, subelite, or rank-and-file in terms of power, wealth, and other preferred outcomes), *myths*, (doctrines, formulas, popular miranda), *techniques* (distribution of operational routines affecting behavior and the resource environment), and *culture materials* (raw resources, processed resources in the environment).

Working within this labyrinth of conditioning factors, the propagandist must depend on his own judgment in assembling, processing, and disseminating his distinctive output, which is a flow of signs that affect what is made available for audiences to focus their attention on. Expressed another way, propaganda activities initiate or take advantage of a network of subsituations in society whose special function is to disseminate and receive (or withhold and reject) messages. The subsituations of 1914–1918 did not include the most distinctive features of today: radio and television networks were either unheard of or had not yet been adapted to propaganda use. The significance of a "forum" (a subsituation specialized in communication) is its potential for rapid and synchronous collective action. In principle, everyone on the globe (or near it), can experience the same event at the same time, and this implies the possibility of acting together with minimum delay.

We are told by neurologists and physiologists that "man's outrageous brain" is composed of a giant johnny-come-lately cortex that is poorly synchronized with the earlier structures of the brain, spinal cord, and gland enzyme system. Hence the malfunctions that find expression in psychosomatic disturbances and behavior disorders. The symbolic component of life proliferates at a rate made possible by the cortical-subcortical systems. Superimposed upon these intraorganic structures of the individual are the new global systems of mass communication. If the cortical-symbolic patterns are full of jerkiness, confusion, and conflict, the situation is exacerbated by a sudden intensification of communication among peoples of contrasting culture, class, interest, and personality and at various levels of crisis in reference to each value-institution sector.

Propagandists themselves take advantage of the opportunity to specialize and to proliferate. They go into business where they are permitted to engage in private enterprise, and they complicate political differences where that is possible. Symbol specialists are promoters who depend on discovering latent responses. Hence they are generators of action, of potential conflict, and this may have positive or negative impacts on the development of a dependable public order in a world whose most obvious feature is lack of it.

Will man learn to live with his cortex? Will he learn to live with his systems of communication? He seems always to have relied on drugs to quiet (as well as to aggravate) his internal condition. And he has traditionally depended on dogmatism and parochialism to prevent change or modify its pace and direction. Under the technoscientific circumstances of today, the ancient tactics would appear to be obsolete, and it is by no means clear whether the basic problems of man on earth will be resolved. The First World War was a sign of destabilization that has since become cumulative and propagandists were busily accentuating every potential for common action, whether destructive or constructive.

2.

IN THE decades since *Propaganda Technique in the World War* was written, it has become less difficult to make a scholarly examination of the process by which policy is formed and executed within specialized agencies of propaganda, as well as of the interplay between such agencies and the principal policy agencies involved in the wider context of wartime decision. Without attempting to provide a systematic contribution to the problems involved, it may at least be rewarding to show how research has gradually improved its chart of the relationships involved in World War I and in the conduct of war in general, especially coalition war.

It will serve to focus the discussion if a generalized model of the political decision process is briefly recapitulated. It must be kept in mind that there is a fundamental distinction between the "decision process" as a "functional" tool of the scholar and scientist and the "conventional" usages current in a given historical situation. The "Emperor" of the German Empire was a conventional participant in the decision process of a major body politic, and the office of Emperor was a recognized organ of authority and control. When we examine the actual impact of the Emperor on the flow of critical decisions we may or may not confirm the popular image. This is what is implied in distinguishing between functional and conventional images: they may or may not prove to be congruent.

The generalized model of a decision process refers to "outcome" events that exist in a continual flow of "preoutcome" and "postoutcome" events. The "participants" in the process include those who take active initiatives to affect results, as well as those who are rather passive responders to the initiatives of others. The "perspectives" of the participants include all the categories of subjectivity (symbols) that in any way affect the power process. The "arenas" are the settings in which interaction takes place. In World War I, for instance, the arenas were more obviously global than they had been even in the Napoleonic era. "Base values" are the assets at the disposal of participants in the arena at any given moment. Hence they include the predispositions favorable to the objectives sought and the resources available for affecting the result. The "strategies" are the techniques by which assets (base values) are utilized to affect outcomes. The "outcomes," as indicated before, are the victories, offsets, or defeats experienced by participants.

It is helpful to expand the "outcome" component of the model to cover seven functional distinctions: *intelligence*, or the giving or withholding of information about plans and occurrences; *promotion*, or the mobilization of policy support; *prescription*, or the crystallization of general objectives and the assignment of means; *invocation*, or the provisional application of prescriptions to concrete circumstances; *application*, or the final application; *termination*, or the ending of prescriptions; *appraisal*, or the assessment of past and present successes or failures.*

Propaganda operations, it is obvious, are promotional activities. A propaganda structure's internal decision process can be examined to show how every function was performed and to explain the causes and consequences of what happened. In the larger perspective of national decision, war propaganda agencies are part of the "application" function, since they operate within the framework of national prescription and all the promotional activities that affect prescription, or any other decision outcome. A given propaganda operation can also be seen as part of interallied decision outcomes (some of which it may in turn affect).

A major question that was not accessible to investigation through research immediately after World War I was the effect of propaganda considerations on the making of high policy during the war. Similarly, the infeasibility of assessing the influence of propaganda considerations in policy formulation made it impossible to investigate its corollary — the manner in which the propaganda process was governed by political decision makers. These two questions are crucial to the development of a comprehensive theory of propaganda, for they

* For more detail, see B.S. Murty, *Propaganda and World Public Order: The Legal Regulation of the Ideological Instrument of Coercion.* New Haven, Conn.: Yale University Press, 1968.

constitute the one point in the process of political communication that is intersected by every other major element of the analytical scheme laid out in *Propaganda Technique in the World War.*

Another way of examining this point of intersection is to look at the concept of war aims. War aims are the political purposes that govern the strategy of warfare and that designate the objectives whose achievement constitutes victory. War aims also determine the nature of the relationship between the policy maker and the propagandist. They are the paramount influence in determining the degree to which propagandists are involved in policy making and the degree to which policy makers are involved in propaganda making. The purpose of the policy maker is to insure that propaganda accurately reflects, and supports the achievement of, a nation's war aims. The purpose of the propagandist is to insure that war aims are formulated in such a way as to insure their maximum exploitation through propaganda.

In another sense, questions as to how the relationships between policy makers and propagandists should be arranged in order to insure optimal cognizance by each of the other's perspective and desiderata are organizational questions. Although *Propaganda Technique* investigated a variety of organizational issues in the conduct of propaganda, it dealt mainly with problems of internal administration (centralization and decentralization, headquarters and field) and lateral coordination (interallied liaison, legislative relations) and touched only lightly on vertical relationships with centers of decision making. That the relationship between policy makers and propagandists was not explored more intensively was the result not only of a dearth of data but also of the fact that the concept of war aims was treated in only one of its many dimensions — as one of the several categories by which the contents of propaganda might be described. War aims possess a more intricate relationship to the propaganda process than is denoted by their incorporation into a typology of content, however, and their role as a functional and analytical linkage between policy, and thus politics, and propaganda needs further elaboration.

In *Propaganda Technique*, war aims were treated simply as one of several types of propaganda content: other major categories were war guilt, satanism, and the illusion of victory. But emphasis on war aims as one category of themes obscures the fact that war aims pervade all categories, for in every category the choice of content is governed by political guide-lines derived from an evolving set of war aims. This does not alter the validity of the categories or imply skepticism about the psychological mechanisms believed to have engendered them, but it does limit the scope of *Propaganda Technique* insofar as it implied that the various types of propaganda were more the spontaneous emanation of mass emotion than the conscious product of the decisions of governments. Although the range of choice for governments is indeed bounded by the "means" and "conditions" of propaganda, significant latitude for the exercise of policy judgment still remains. And although it may be true that nations at war will exploit ineluctably the notions of war guilt, the illusion of victory, and satanism, there will be substantial differences in how and to what degree those themes are exploited, differences that will in turn derive from the nature of a nation's war aims.

The experience of the United States in 1918 as compared with its allies in the Entente is illustrative. In its war guilt propaganda, the Entente made an indiscriminate and comprehensive indictment of the German nation for causing the war, while the United States restricted its condemnation of Germany to its military leaders and specifically exculpated the mass of the German people. In maintaining the illusion of victory, the propaganda of the Entente more or less explicitly envisaged so thorough a triumph over Germany as to entail its virtual subjugation, while the United States contemplated, if not exactly a peace without victory, then certainly a moderate peace after an unequivocal if humane victory. In the propaganda of satanism, the attitude of the Entente could be summed up in the phrase, "Hang the Kaiser," while the propaganda of the United States conspicuously exempted both the person and the institution of the Emperor as objects for attack. In each case, the differences in the propaganda of the Entente are attributable less to "means" and "conditions" than to the differences that existed between the war aims of the United States and those of its allies.

Closer examination of the range of choice open to propagandists further illuminates the function of policy in the selection of content. In the conduct of war guilt propaganda, for instance, the range of possibilities about who is guilty is a wide one: a political party, an individual, a class, an ethnic group, a region, an elite, a set of institutions, a social movement, an ideology, a political system, or any combination of these. The criteria of the propagandist will reduce the realm of choice considerably, but enough alternatives will probably remain so that the propagandist will need the guidance of the policy maker to tell him which among them are the most appropriate and effective objects for the attachment of guilt. This kind of operational imperative creates a need for political guidance of even those aspects of propaganda that seem devoid of political content, referents, or implications.

In such a context, the category of war aims itself takes on a somewhat fuller meaning. It is further differentiated from other categories by the fact that it is the most highly political in both substance and significance. Thus, it is the one that is apt to receive the most attention from policy makers and, as a result, is also the one that is likely to offer the most limited opportunities for manipulation by the propagandist. The policy guidelines rendered by the decision maker will be most direct, continuous, and explicit with reference to the propaganda of war aims, and that guidance will be doubly constraining both as a "means" and as a "condition." The motive of the policy maker in issuing this guidance — to insure that propaganda is consistent with policy — is an incentive that produces additional benefits for the internal processes of propaganda. Hence, if the structure of war aims has been clearly delineated by higher political authority, the propagandist is able to manage policy questions relating to the other categories largely by inference, thereby reducing the need for equally close guidance on them.

Moreover, it is not enough to point out that war aims are the link connecting the propaganda process to all the other operations that constitute the conduct of a war. It is also necessary to specify how the manifestation of war aims in other aspects of warfare relates to the propaganda of war aims. Obviously, war aims are not a construct devised solely or even primarily for the guidance or convenience of the propagandist. War aims are a matrix of political and diplomatic objectives which interweave strategies of propaganda with all the strategies — military, economic, and others — pursued by a country at war. They are not merely the specification of post-war purposes or an adroit selection of issues and symbols with which to enlist wartime sympathies. They are also the definition of a political field, the selection of an organizational and political strategy, an identification of friends and enemies and neutrals, not only among states, but among all the constituent groups within states. War aims not only build and maintain coalitions between nations; more important, they create coalitions among subnational groups — whether allied, neutral, or enemy — with common interests transcending national boundaries. In a sense, propaganda is the extension and elaboration of an organizational strategy through the communication of symbols. That is to say, properly conceived the problem of organization in propaganda extends beyond the forms and mechanics employed within propaganda agencies for the production of political communications. It also embraces the extragovernmental effort by government to structure and relate groups and private persons in ways that will allow propaganda to obtain maximum reverberation throughout the social system or systems addressed. More than any other category of content, the propaganda of war aims is the catalyst of transnational political action.

All of these considerations are complicated substantially when the problems involved in the communication of war aims to each of the principal audiences of propaganda — home, enemy, neutral, and allied — are added to the numerous

implications of war aims as a set of themes, as guidance on all themes, and as a network of strategies. The character and effect of war aims propaganda varies significantly, depending on which audience is addressed. Despite the complexities already referred to, it is nonetheless easier to manage the propaganda of war aims to home, enemy, and neutral audiences than to coordinate the war aims propaganda of allies.
. The propaganda of war aims to home audiences, though susceptible to periodic political crisis, is seldom vulnerable to continuous or massive challenge from within. Similarly, neutral opinion is rarely a crucial factor in the management of war aims propaganda. Moreover, although war aims are theoretically of supreme importance between enemies, the total, ideological nature of twentieth-century warfare has rendered war aims rigid and ritualistic, more a heraldic device than a diplomatic agenda. The bargaining functions of belligerent war aims have been transformed from a dialogue between regimes into the mutual subversion of them. As a result, the propaganda of war aims to enemies is less a means of achieving their reconciliation, or even their destruction, than a means for consolidating and maintaining the unity of allies.

Indeed, the most crucial referent for the propaganda of war aims would seem to be a nation's allies, for it is only in undertaking to coordinate propaganda with allies that the element of consent is injected into the process of propaganda. The formal consensual elements present in propaganda to neutrals are extremely limited so long as it is unilateral, and there are none in propaganda to enemy audiences. However, any effort among allies in a coalition to coordinate propaganda to enemies or neutrals requires agreement among the participants. That an alliance needs to preserve a united front on policy would seem to be a self-evident proposition, in all likelihood an inevitable concomitant of coalition warfare.

It is not overly difficult for alliance partners holding disparate purposes to agree on how to employ — or to reconcile disagreements on how to employ — propaganda falling in the categories of war guilt, satanism, or the illusion of victory. Although each of these categories implies or embodies a national position on war aims, the incidence of major policy problems over them is surprisingly infrequent, probably because they are usually camouflaged from mass perception by emphases on quite different, more vivid symbols. However, it is much more difficult for allies to harmonize their policies or muffle their disagreements on the propaganda of war aims. Something of the magnitude of the complexities involved is indicated by the fact that the effort made in World War I to coordinate allied propaganda failed so resoundingly that the effort was not made at all in World War II. Although it may be argued that the propaganda of war aims was regarded as of considerable importance in World War II, this was true only in a negative sense, for the adoption of the policy of unconditional surrender at the beginning of 1943 had the practical effect of nullifying all such issues for the rest of the war.

Yet even the experience of failure was sufficient to demonstrate how many of the processes of propaganda and diplomacy merge in Allied attempts to collaborate on propaganda and how useful that area of overlap is as a focus of analysis. For if war aims themes are the crucial category of content, and allies are the crucial audience referent, then it follows that a comparative study of the war aims propaganda of allies should constitute the analytical nexus of the policy, the politics, and the propaganda of coalition warfare. The comparative approach to the communications of conflict opens broad theoretical perspectives on the study of propaganda (which become broader still when propaganda between internally and externally competitive coalitions is compared) and maintains the "operational" orientation so desirable as a bridge to related fields of inquiry.

Such strong emphasis has been placed on war aims not for analytical reasons alone but also because the propaganda of World War I was preeminently a propaganda of war aims. In relation to other categories of content, the category of war aims was much larger in the First World War than it was in the other major conflicts of modern history. Indeed, since *Propaganda Technique in the World War* was published, the best pertinent historical scholarship has not been explicitly devoted to propaganda but rather has consisted of political and diplomatic studies of the dynamics of the competing war aims of the great powers. Outstanding examples of this aspect of the literature are such titles as: Victor S. Mamatey, *The United States and East Central Europe: A Study in Wilsonian Diplomacy and Propaganda* (Princeton: Princeton University Press, 1957); George F. Kennan, *Soviet-American Relations, 1917–1920*, 2 vols. (Princeton: Princeton University Press, 1956–1958); and Fritz Fisher, *Germany's Aims in the First World War* (New York: W. W. Norton, 1967). More synoptic treatments are contained in N. Gordon Levin, Jr., *Woodrow Wilson and World Politics: America's Response to War and Revolution* (New York: Oxford University Press, 1968) and

Arno J. Mayer, *Political Origins of the New Diplomacy, 1917–1918* (New Haven: Yale University Press, 1958).

Although there has been a renaissance of interest in the First World War during the past fifteen years as archival material has become progressively more available, the production of historical studies dealing with propaganda has been perhaps less voluminous than was anticipated at the time *Propaganda Technique* appeared. Most subsequent studies of propaganda in World War I were published during the 1930s as the tides of revisionism swept through the scholarly output of Europe and the United States. Thus, with few exceptions, these studies are parochial in character and orthodox in approach, marked with the residue of the First World War and the imminence of the second, deprived of adequate documentation and antedating contemporary methodological sophistication in communications research. Typically, they deal with the contents and the effects of propaganda, with a secondary emphasis on the organization and operation of propaganda agencies. They reflect an inordinate preoccupation with Germany and the United States as audiences for propaganda. However, none of these studies seems to alter significantly the theoretical structure or any of the individual propositions put forward in *Propaganda Technique*.

Among the works devoted to the American audience, H.C. Peterson, *Propaganda for War: The Campaign against American Neutrality, 1914–1917* (Norman: University of Oklahoma Press, 1939), James Duane Squires, *British Propaganda at Home and in The United States: From 1914 to 1917* (Cambridge: Harvard University Press, 1935), and Albert R. Buchanan, "European Propaganda and American Public Opinion," (Ph.D.

thesis, Stanford University, 1935), deal with British and German competition for American opinion, while Fred A. Sonderman, "The Wilson Administration's Image of Germany," (Ph.D. thesis, Yale University, 1953), treats an important attitudinal condition affecting that propaganda competition. James R. Mock and Cedric Larson, *Words That Won the War: The Story of the Committee on Public Information, 1917–1919* (Princeton, N.J.: Princeton University Press, 1939), is mainly a description of the domestic propaganda of the American government after it had become a belligerent. Supplementing this is Walton E. Bean, "George Creel and His Critics: A Study of the Attacks on the Committee on Public Information," (Ph.D. thesis, University of California, Berkeley, 1941), which examines several of the larger controversies that arose in the course of Creel's domestic work. Among the best of the American-focused studies is David Wayne Hirst, "German Propaganda in the United States, 1914–1917," (Ph.D. thesis, Northwestern University, 1962).

Among the studies investigating the German audience, Erwin Weiss, *Die Propaganda der Vereinigten Staaten gegen Deutschland im Ersten Weltkrieg* (Essen: Essener Verlag, 1943), and Gotthard Scholz, "Staatliche Information und Propaganda im Krieg: Das U.S. Committee on Public Information (1917–1919)" (dissertation, Heidelberg University, 1967; the only German work to utilize United States archives extensively), deal with American propaganda against Germany. Georg Huber, *Die französische Propaganda im Weltkrieg gegen Deutschland, 1914 bis 1918* (Munich: Dr. F. A. Pfeiffer, 1928), supplements the earlier memoir on the subject by Hansi [Johann Jakob Waltz] and E. Tonnelat. Three works examine the Entente's propaganda against Germany: Wilhelm Ernst, *Die anti-deutsche Propaganda durch das Schweizer Gebiet im Weltkrieg, speziell die Propaganda in Bayern* (Munich, 1933); Hans Thimme, *Weltkrieg ohne Waffen: Die Propaganda der Westmächte gegen Deutschland, ihre Wirkung und ihre Abwehr* (Stuttgart and Berlin: Cotta, 1932); and George G. Bruntz, *Allied Propaganda and the Collapse of the German Empire in 1918* (Stanford: Stanford University Press, 1938).

Also noteworthy are two analytic studies: Arthur Ponsonby, *Falsehood in War-time* (New York: Dutton, 1928) and James M. Read, *Atrocity Propaganda, 1914–1919* (New Haven: Yale University Press, 1941).

Though none of these works illuminates the interrelationships of policy and propaganda, the implicit assumption of *Propaganda Technique in the World War* that policymakers were significantly influenced in their political decisions by considerations of propaganda and public opinion and deeply involved in their management appears quite valid in light of research currently in progress regarding decision making in American propaganda abroad during World War I.* This research indicates that a strong awareness of the importance of propaganda and public opinion pervaded the highest echelons of government in the United States and permits the speculation that this may have been equally true of other belligerent governments.

Illustrative of the kind of intimacy that existed between policy and propaganda are the procedures employed in the

---

* The junior author of this introduction is preparing studies on American psychological warfare against enemy forces on the Western front and on the linkages between the idea of open diplomacy and its expression by agencies of the government through propaganda abroad.

preparation of propaganda pamphlets by the temporary war-time agency for official propaganda, the Committee on Public Information. The committee both originated and received suggestions on subjects suitable for propaganda treatment in pamphlet form, and the most worthwhile among them were passed to its director, George Creel. After further winnowing, Creel would take the ones that remained to President Wilson for the selection of topics and for guidance on their treatment. Galley proofs of the pamphlet would be sent to the Secretary of State and then to the President for revision and final approval before being printed and distributed. From the perspective of half a century, it seems scarcely credible that a chief of state would play such an extraordinarily direct role in the preparation of propaganda. Yet, for a man who wrote all of his own speeches, encrypted and deciphered many of his own most sensitive cables, and habitually composed diplomatic notes at his own typewriter, as Wilson did, it is perhaps not as astounding as it seems.

The Army's propaganda leaflets were produced in an equally unusual manner. As the general staff of the Army prepared in the spring of 1918 to undertake leaflet propaganda against enemy forces, it recognized a need to obtain authoritative interpretation of United States war aims for the guidance of its propagandists. Finding the State Department neither capable of nor willing to render this guidance, the Army turned to the Inquiry, the scholarly research organization set up at Wilson's order under the supervision of his closest adviser, Col. Edward M. House, to formulate American war aims and relate them to European conditions and war aims. Formal arrangements were made between the Inquiry and the Military Intelligence

Section of the general staff, which was responsible for military propaganda, whereby the academic experts staffing the Inquiry would actually draft the propaganda leaflets to be distributed at the front. After leaving the Inquiry, the drafts were to be personally reviewed by Secretary of War Newton D. Baker before being released for distribution in France. Although these arrangements later proved unworkable, their intention was achieved by means of a quite different device. Military Intelligence commissioned and sent to France one of the principal officers of the Inquiry, Walter Lippmann, to act as the political adviser and chief leaflet writer and editor for the propaganda unit of the American Expeditionary Forces. Because of Lippmann's knowledge of the work of the Inquiry, with which he retained official ties, and his personal connections with Col. House, the Army was able to achieve great fidelity to policy in its propaganda leaflets.

To what degree this American sensitivity to foreign opinion and propaganda was shared by the other belligerents is a question whose answers lie in the archives of Europe. As the search for them proceeds, scholars will no doubt continue to regard Lasswell's seminal *Propaganda Technique in the World War* not only as an "incisive common-sense analysis" but as the "outstanding contribution in any language to the history of the subject."*

July 1970

---

* Ralph Haswell Lutz, "Studies of World War Propaganda, 1914–1933," *Journal of Modern History* 5 (1933): 496–497.

PROPAGANDA TECHNIQUE
IN WORLD WAR I

CHAPTER I

THE MATTER IN HAND

THERE are abundant signs of interest in international propaganda since the War of 1914. Several books have been published by men who held responsible propaganda posts during the War. Creel in the United States, Stuart in England, Nicolai in Germany, and Waitz and Tonnelet in France, have published much of their record to the world. Individual propaganda agents of high and low degree have written their memoirs, and international propaganda is alluded to in every reminiscence and apology of post-armistice times.

The professors and the graduate students and the publicists have swollen the flood of systematic speculation about, and systematic examination of, the subject. Among the conspicuous names in Germany, where the best work has been done, are Johann Plenge, Edgar Stern-Rubarth, Ferdinand Tönnies, and Kurt Baschwitz.[1] Research monographs of some value have been prepared by Schönemann, who wrote in German on the United States, Marchand,

[1] For the titles of their books, and the writings referred to elsewhere in this chapter, see the bibliography.

1

who wrote in French on certain aspects of German propaganda, Wiehler, who wrote in German on special problems, and several others. Démartial dissected his own French and Allied propaganda during the War in a brilliant contribution to the de-bunking of world opinion. Members of the new propaganda, or publicity, profession have begun to rationalize their own practices. The books by Bernays and Wilder and Buell are pioneers in this direction. Universities have begun to offer courses of lectures upon the new technique, and vast collections of War propaganda have been assembled at Stuttgart, Paris, London and Stanford.

There are many reasons why the rôle of propaganda in international politics, and especially in war-time, is receiving more careful scrutiny to-day than heretofore. There is a new inquisitiveness abroad in the world. Some of the people who in the years before the War were disposed to accept the changing tides of international animosity and friendship as inevitable manifestations of the cosmic fate, which commanded the sun to rise or the rain to fall, have become suspicious of the supernatural or the impersonal character of these events. A word has appeared, which has come to have an ominous clang in many minds —Propaganda. We live among more people than ever, who are puzzled, uneasy, or vexed at the unknown cunning which seems to have duped and degraded them. It is often an object of vituperation, and therefore, of interest, discussion and, finally, of study.

These people probe the mysteries of propaganda with that compound of admiration and chagrin with which the victims of a new gambling trick demand to have the thing explained. That credulous utopianism, which fed upon the mighty words which exploited the hopes of the mass in war, has in many minds given way to cynicism and disenchantment, and with these earnest souls propaganda is a far more serious matter. Some of those who trusted so much and hated so passionately have put their hands to the killing of man, they have mutilated others and perhaps been mutilated in return, they have encouraged others to draw the sword, and they have derided and besmirched those who refused to rage as they did. Fooled by propaganda? If so, they writhe in the knowledge that they were the blind pawns in plans which they did not incubate, and which they neither devised nor comprehended nor approved.

In the defeated countries, such as Germany, the military people have seized upon propaganda to save their own faces. They declare that their army was never defeated by the battering of Allied battalions, but that the nation collapsed behind their lines because all the alien and radical elements in the population were easy marks for the seductive bait of foreign propaganda. This is plausible to the public because people were everywhere warned during the war to beware the noxious fumes of enemy propaganda. The Germans were wrought up over " Reuter, the fabricator of War lies," Northcliffe, " The Minister of Lying," and the Allies, the " All-lies." They were, therefore, predisposed to attach very great importance to propaganda. Since the War Germany has been shorn of military strength, and must, therefore, rely upon subtler means of protecting and advancing its interests than armed coercion. Patriotic

Germans are anxious to understand the nature of the non-coercive weapon which was wielded so successfully to their discomfiture in war-time, and there is to-day a more luxurious flowering of treatises upon international propaganda (its nature, limitations and processes) in Germany than anywhere else.

In some measure the present occupation with propaganda is due to the outright pacifists. There is a widespread belief that fighting is due to ill-will, and that, if war is to cease, there must be a " moratorium on hate." Can propaganda furnish a weapon of direct attack upon the psychology of nations, and expose the ways and means of sowing confidence where mistrust rankles?

This whole discussion about the ways and means of controlling public opinion testifies to the collapse of the traditional species of democratic romanticism and to the rise of a dictatorial habit of mind. As long as the democrats were in opposition, they were free to belabour the fact of an infallible though almighty king with the fantasy of an all-wise public. Enthrone the public and dethrone the king! Pass the sceptre to the wise!

Familiarity with the ruling public has bred contempt. Modern reflections upon democracy boil down to the proposition, more or less contritely expressed, that the democrats were deceiving themselves. The public has not reigned with benignity and restraint. The good life is not in the mighty rushing wind of public sentiment. It is no organic secretion of the horde, but the tedious achievement of the few. The lover of the good life no longer consults Sir Oracle; he pulls the strings of Punch and

Judy. Thus argues the despondent democrat. Let us, therefore, reason together, brethren, he sighs, and find the good, and when we have found it, let us find out how to make up the public mind to accept it. Inform, cajole, bamboozle and seduce in the name of the public good. Preserve the majority convention, but dictate to the majority !

To the sombre curiosity of the discouraged democrat must be added the analytical motive of the social scientist. The division of social thinking has at last reached a point which enables a few people to achieve a fixed preoccupation with the explanation of how the social wheels go round, wholly apart from any pressing anxiety to steer them in any particular direction. Their business is to discover and report, not to philosophize and reform. They are more anxious to gratify their curiosity than to follow the footsteps of the deity who created man in his own image.

The people who probe the mysteries of public opinion in 'politics must, for the present, at least, rely upon something other than exact measurement, to confirm or discredit their speculations. Generalizations about public opinion stick because they are plausible and not because they are experimentally established. They fall by the wayside, when others, who have had experience with the kind of fact which they purport to describe, disagree with the original observer. Sometimes this disagreement is sharp and emphatic, because it comes from people who have tried to use existing notions about public opinion in their efforts to control it. This is the engineering test. It is employed by propagandists and publicity-men of all sorts and shapes.

Conjectures in the field of public opinion are particularly

susceptible to engineering tests.   But much of the literature of public opinion is of such abstruse and indefinite character that it defies empirical verification.   There is a plethora of theories about something known as public opinion in general, and a paucity of hypotheses about public opinions in particular.   When the field of public opinion is split into the problems of explaining and controlling opinions about policies, attitudes toward persons and groups, and attitudes toward the various modes of political participation, some more tangible progress may be expected.

The rôle of opinion in international politics is peculiarly worthy of study, because it is a matter of growing importance. We are witnessing the growth of a world public, and this public has arisen in part, because international propaganda has at once agitated and organized it.   Interests overlap boundaries.   It is a mere fiction that the citizens and the governments of each country refrain from meddling in affairs which are technically within the competence of another.   In the summer of 1925, for instance, the German Reichstag was engaged in considering a proposal to levy protective duties upon agricultural and manufactured commodities.   Theoretically, this is a domestic question, and is reserved for the exclusive determination of whoever happens to live inside the boundaries of the juristic entity called Germany.   But in point of fact, external interests were affected, and they brought pressure to bear in their own behalf.   American manufacturers, whose goods would be barred if the tariff went into operation, joined forces with British, French and German interests and sent their agents to Germany.   They sought to reach the Press and to strengthen the hands of the elements inside Germany, who stood out against the bill.

Such private influencing as this is no longer the exception, but the custom. Corporations, for instance, find it convenient to subsidize newspapers abroad ; and influencing is by no means confined to unofficial persons. Governments take an active hand in the game. The prestige-propaganda of the Japanese on the exclusion question, the " myth of a single guilty nation " propaganda of the Germans against the Versailles settlement, and the Soviet propaganda for American recognition are current cases. The new organs of international government are in close touch with interests inside each nation. The International Labour Office co-operates with those who wish to procure the ratification and the enforcement of the draft conventions of the International Labour Conference.

Official propaganda often takes the form of encouraging patriotic societies with branches abroad. The League of Germans Abroad claims to have 150 locals in Germany and in foreign countries, and the Union for Germanism Abroad says that it has over a million members in Germany and Austria. There are special organizations for Austria, Schleswig, the Saar Territory, Danzig, Czecho-Slovakia, Poland, the Tyrol, the Danube and overseas. These associations exist to keep alive a sentiment of cultural unity and may, in times of emergency, go further.

Governments smile benevolently upon certain international societies, such as the *Alliance Francaise* and the English-Speaking Union. They keep open channels of influence, which may be valuable in times of strain.

There are innumerable official and unofficial propagandas to instigate revolution, secession, or racial, cultural, geographical and religious unity. Such are suggested by these words : Communism, Irish Independence, Pan-Islam, Pan-Slav, Pan-America, Pan-Europe, League of Nations Union. There are propagandas on behalf of political personalities, for it is important to procure a favourable reception for every ambassador at a new post.

It is public opinion and propaganda in war-time which calls forth the most strenuous exertions. The conduct of war, conceived as a psychological problem, may be stated in terms of moral. A nation with a high moral is capable of performing the tasks laid upon it because of a certain momentum, which can only be measured when serious resistances appear. The conventional signs of high moral are enthusiasm, determination, self-confidence, absence of carping criticism and absence of complaint. Almost every fact may have its implication for moral. The calories in the official ration, the supply of cigarettes, the opportunities for recreation, the confidence of officers and public men, the smart demeanour of the troops, the mode of inflicting discipline ; all this, and more, affects the fighting vim and tenacity of the military and civil population.

The problem of maintaining moral is only in part a problem of propaganda, because propaganda is but one of the many devices which must be relied upon. Its scope is limited though important. By propaganda is not meant the control of mental states by changing such objective conditions as the supply of cigarettes or the chemical composition of food. Propaganda does not even include the stiffening of moral by a cool and confident bearing. It refers solely to the control of opinion by significant symbols, or, to speak more concretely and less accurately, by stories, rumours, reports, pictures and other forms of social communication. Propaganda is concerned with the management of opinions and attitudes by the direct manipulation of social suggestion rather than by altering other conditions in the environment or in the organism.

Propaganda is one of the three chief implements of operation against a belligerent enemy :—

Military Pressure (The coercive power of the land, sea and air forces).

Economic Pressure (Interference with access to sources of material, markets, capital and labour power).

Propaganda (Direct use of suggestion).

Negotiation is a method of influencing foreign states with which one is not in active combat. By negotiation is meant the official exchanges which look toward agreement. Mediation between contending parties and submission to arbitration are both commonly invoked. A government influences its own people by legislation, adjudication, policing, propaganda, and ceremonialism. For the soldiers, whom it has under the most complete control, it must make adequate provision of necessities and relaxation on pain of trouble. It drills them into a unified missile of destruction.

During war much reliance must be placed on propaganda to promote economy of food, textiles, fuel, and other commodities, and to stimulate recruiting, employment in war industries, service in relief work, and the purchase of bonds. But by far the most potent rôle of propaganda is to mobilize the animosity of the community against the enemy, to maintain friendly relations with neutrals and allies, to arouse the neutrals against the enemy, and to break up the solid wall of enemy antagonism.   In short, it is the significance of propaganda for international attitudes in war which renders it of peculiar importance.

International war propaganda rose to such amazing dimensions in the last war, because the communization of warfare necessitated the mobilization of the civilian mind. No government could hope to win without a united nation behind it, and no government could have a united nation behind it unless it controlled the minds of its people.   The civilians had to be depended upon to supply recruits for the front and for the war industries.   The sacrifices of war had to be borne without complaints that spread dissension at home and discouragement in the trenches.

Now the civilians cannot be subjected to the same discipline as the soldiers.   The effect of the drill to which the soldier is subjected is thus described by Maxwell :—

> the individual becomes highly imitative, conforming his movements in every respect to those of the drill-sergeants. He is not permitted to make the slightest alteration in the movements which he is shown, and is stopped again and again until at last his movements are satisfactory. At this stage in a soldier's training his behaviour is almost mechanical, and the unity achieved throughout the group is very little higher than that displayed by a machine. . . . The mere fact that each man acts like his neighbour enables the individual to rely upon the co-operation of his fellows with reference to the common end. On the

parade ground each man soon discovers that every member of his unit is co-operating with him in the evolution in progress.   In the trenches he is confident that the men on either side of him are doing the same, and that the divisions on the flanks of his own divisions are co-operating for the common end.   It is through discipline that it is achieved (this co-operation) in the Army, and the mutual trust engendered has the effect of welding what might otherwise be only a mechanical organization into a living unity.[1]

Active service brings with it a tendency to relapse to the primitive.   Many observers have said that it is the simple bed-rock things that matter most.   It is food and drink and smokes and sleep and warmth and shelter and creature comforts that bulk largest at the front.   The human values and sentiments are left to atrophy for want of stimulation.   The quiet influence of the presence of friendly scenes and faces is lost.   The influence of certain of the more complex forms of religion is less.[2]

Military life approximates the aggregation of disciplined men in a dehumanizing environment.   The civilian lacks the automatic discipline of drill and remains in an environment in which his sentiment-life (his *human* life) continues. Civilian unity is not achieved by the regimentation of muscles.   It is achieved by a repetition of ideas rather than movements.   The civilian mind is standardized by news and not by drills.   Propaganda is the method by which this process is aided and abetted.

The intentional circulation of ideas by propaganda helps to overcome the psychic resistances to whole-hearted participation in war, which have arisen with the decay of personal

[1] *A Psychological Retrospect of the Great War*, p. 162.
[2] See Maxwell, as cited, 100.

loyalty to chiefs. Peace has come to be regarded as the normal state of society, and not war. There are ideologies which condemn war either as something bad in itself, or as the product of a detested order of society. Propaganda is the war of ideas on ideas.

This study is a preliminary and highly provisional analysis of the group of propaganda problems connected with the control of international antipathies and attractions in wartime. How may hate be mobilized against an enemy? How may the enemy be demoralized by astute manipulation? How is it possible to cement the friendship of neutral and allied peoples?

It is not proposed to write history, but to describe technique. When the war has receded further into the past, it will be possible to write at least a fragmentary history of the international propaganda of the time. The aim of the present inquiry is at once more modest and more ambitious than this. It is more modest in that it has chosen but a few of the facts which will be included in a comprehensive history. It is more ambitious in that it has undertaken to evolve an explicit theory of how international war propaganda may be conducted with success. It relies almost exclusively upon American, British, French and German experience.

Why not postpone the theory of method until the history is finished? The answer is that we knew enough about the history to justify a provisional study of technique, and a technical study at this time will perhaps improve the quality of the forthcoming history. After all, the relation between the student whose main interest is in the mechanism and the student whose chief concern is what happened in a particular circumstance is reciprocal. In a sense, the scientist and the engineer ask questions for the historian to answer, and the historian reports upon the probable influence of specific factors in a definite set of past circumstances. The lines are never mutually exclusive, for the historian is continually uncovering a new example of method, while the technical student is often able to plug a gap in chronology through his researches.

The procedure in this investigation has been to stick close to common-sense analysis. There are many seductive analogies between collective behaviour and the behaviour of individuals in a clinic,[1] but the analogies are too easily strained in the making. Clinical psychology is too rudimentary to carry an imposing superstructure. The present study goes no further than to develop a simple classification of the various psychological materials, which have been used to produce certain specified results, and to propose a general theory of strategy and tactics, for the manipulation of these materials. Subsequent inquiry and criticism may find other categories which are at once more accurate and suggestive.

[1] See, for example, Miss Playne's book called *The Neuroses of Nations.*

CHAPTER II

PROPAGANDA ORGANIZATION

INSIDE a democratic country there is a certain presumption against government propaganda. As Representative Gillett, commenting upon the Creel Bureau, said, admitting that it has not been conducted in a partisan spirit :

> That is the great danger of such a bureau as this, because we must all admit that if any administration has in its power a Bureau of Public Information, as it is called, but really an advertising bureau, a propaganda bureau, a bureau of publicity, to exploit the various acts and departments of the Government, it is a very dangerous thing in a Republic ; because, if used in a partisan spirit or for partisan advantage of the administration, it has tremendous power, and in ordinary peace-time I do not think any party or any administration would justify it or approve it.[1]

The truth is that all governments are engaged to some extent in propaganda as part of their ordinary peace-time functions. They make propaganda on behalf of diplomatic friends or against diplomatic antagonists, and this is unavoidable. While, therefore, the presumption exists against propaganda work by a democratic government, this statement should not be taken too literally.

During the war-period it came to be recognized that the mobilization of men and means was not sufficient ; there must be a mobilization of opinion. Power over opinion,

---

[1] *U.S. Cong. Rec.*, 65th Cong., 2nd Sess., p. 7915.

as over life and property, passed into official hands, because the danger from licence was greater than the danger of abuse.   Indeed, there is no question but that government management of opinion is an unescapable corollary of large-scale modern war.   The only question is the degree to which the government should try to conduct its propaganda secretly, and the degree to which it should conduct it openly. As far as the home public is concerned, there is nothing to be gained by concealment, and there is a certain loss of prestige for all that is said, when secrecy is attempted.   The carrying power of ideas is greatly increased when the authority of the government is added to them.   With certain insignificant exceptions (the smuggling of propaganda material into adjacent enemy countries), nothing is lost, if all propaganda operations in neutral and allied countries are carried on openly.   Otherwise, indeed, suspicion and distrust may exist where complete confidence and understanding are indispensable.   The United States Committee on Public Information was undoubtedly correct in notifying neutral governments of what they wanted to do inside neutral borders.

It is bad tactics, however, to announce blatantly to the enemy that a " Director of Propaganda in Enemy Countries " has been named.   As Sir Herbert Samuel said in the House of Commons, when Lord Northcliffe was appointed to this post in 1918 :

> Possibly the Germans may regard Lord Northcliffe, the proprietor of the *Daily Mail* and the *Evening News*, in much the same light as we may regard Count Reventlow. What should we think, if we heard that an official announcement had been made by the German Government, that they

had appointed Count Reventlow as the Director to carry on propaganda in the United Kingdom, and in other Allied countries ? [1]

Assuming, in principle, that propaganda should be conducted in the open by a belligerent government, the problem of organization presents itself. What agencies should carry on the work, and to what degree is unity of command practicable ? The work of carrying on the war brings several government services into the active control of certain streams of information, and international attitudes are to some degree involved with the rest. There is the Foreign Office at home, and the Diplomatic and Consular staffs abroad. There is the War and Naval Department at home, and the Military and Naval Attachés abroad. There is the General Staff and the Field Headquarters. There are the various service ministries engaged upon problems of supply and internal regulation. The mere enumeration of these agencies is sufficient to remind one of the evident proposition that the influencing of attitudes is implicit in every function, and that it is incapable of complete segregation in anything like the degree to which, let us say, the purchasing of horses can be confined to a particular agency.

Disunity brings dangers. The Foreign Office and the Field Headquarters may hold out contradictory inducements to the enemy and cast the whole propaganda of demoralization into disrepute. The military people at home may announce the destruction of public buildings in the occupied zone, much to the consternation of the diplomatic representa-

---

[1] 103 *H. C. Deb*, 5s., col. 1410, 27 February, 1918.

tives in neutral countries. There is always the possibility that bad news of different kinds may break simultaneously and produce an unwonted state of depression if each service gives its own news to the public.   The news of a naval loss, a military loss and an aviation loss may come when there is a shortage of flour, and when there is a prickly set of wage and price problems agitating the prints at home.   If this news were handled through a central clearing house, it could be distributed over a period of time and nullified by the more favourable aspects of the general situation.

Disunity leads to a considerable duplication of effort.   If the military people publish the same pamphlet that the diplomatic service publishes, and distribute it through the military attachés abroad when the diplomatic attachés have already doled it out, no good purpose can be served. It is difficult to work out a revision of general policy in the light of propaganda efforts, where there is no continuing mechanism for keeping tab on the whole range of propaganda work.   The backwardness of certain departments, which may be opposed to publicity, may produce a repercussion of uneasiness and distrust.   There may be delay in shifting the personnel devoted to propaganda work to the sectors where the most effect can be secured.

Some of these dangers may be offset by the dangers of unity.   Any scheme of unity runs the risk of antagonizing the *amour propre* of some service and of ruining moral.   If the control of foreign and domestic propaganda were integrated too tightly in the hands of one man, the one or the other might suffer from the preconceptions of the responsible head.   Their requirements are so different that only a rare combination of talents can be relied upon to develop both of them to the highest efficiency.

The balance seems to point toward unity as more desirable than disunity, but it seems to justify a scheme of organization which preserves a considerable degree of autonomy to the constituent services. What are the possible forms of organization? There might be a single propaganda executive. There might be a committee of executives, each responsible for some branch of propaganda work, such as propaganda against the enemy, propaganda in neutral and allied countries, propaganda among civilians, and propaganda in the fighting forces. In any case, the propaganda work in training camps, at the front, in rest camps, on shipboard, and in transit, would vest largely in the military and naval authorities. A third method is to arrange a common Press conference for all departments, but to leave all other forms of effort to the regular agencies affected, which would especially be the Foreign Office, General Headquarters, the War Department, and the Ministry of the Interior. Broadly speaking, the United States adopted the first expedient in the last war, Great Britain, the second, and Germany, the third.

A Committee on Public Information was appointed, by order of the President, soon after the entrance of the United States into the War. It was composed of the Secretaries of the Navy and War Departments, the Secretary of State, and Mr. George Creel. This was equivalent to appointing a separate cabinet member for propaganda, in fact, and Mr. Creel was responsible for every aspect of propaganda work, both at home and abroad. One result of this method of organization was to confer upon the representatives of the Committee abroad something of the prestige of three great government departments, and to satisfy the self-esteem of each one.

While the American system sprang into existence at a single stroke, and remained substantially unaltered during the War, the British system went through a long and intricate series of changes. As Major-General Sir George Aston wrote :

> Party politicians are suspicious folk, unwilling to trust any Government with money to spend on propaganda, for fear that they will spend it in their own interest rather than the country's. So the Parliamentary War Aims Committee was established with representatives of all parties. The Committee was charged with Home Propaganda, and came in for much criticism.[1]

A small department was set up at Wellington House in the office of the Insurance Commissioners to prepare pamphlets and leaflets. Wellington House initiated the Bryce Report, which was one of the triumphs of the War, on the propaganda front, but most of its material was put out as though it were a private and not an official agency. A films and wireless committee was later set up under Mr. Mair, but its relation to the Home Office and the Foreign Office was uncertain. A Press Bureau was improvised in August, 1914, and was later adopted by the Home Office. The Foreign Office was meanwhile engaged in the following activities, according to a statement in Parliament by the Under-Secretary of State for Foreign Affairs (Mr. Acland) :

[1] " Propaganda and the Father of It," *Cornhill Magazine*, N.S., v. 48 : 233–241.

We are taking steps to see that there is supplied to the Press in neutral countries not only news strictly so-called, but also news which we take here to be rather commonplace, but which is of real interest to other countries, as to the condition of this country, and information with regard to trade, and with regard to employment, and with regard to recruiting, and with regard to all such matters as to which the condition of this country is really of interest to our friends.[1]

In January, 1917, the Department of Information was organized. Colonel Buchan had charge of four widely scattered services, and was responsible to the war Cabinet and the Prime Minister. An Advisory Committee was established, which consisted of Lord Northcliffe, Lord Burnham, Mr. Robert Donald, and Mr. C. P. Scott. When Lord Northcliffe proceeded on his mission to America, Lord Beaverbrook was appointed to this Committee, and later, Sir George Riddell was added. Things were still at loose ends under this system, and Sir E. Carson, a member of the War Cabinet, was asked to co-ordinate the various agencies. The War Department had organized a separate service for the purpose of conducting propaganda against the German Army, and the civilian peoples. Finally, in February, 1918, Lord Beaverbrook was made Minister of Information, occupying the post of Chancellor of the Duchy of Lancaster. At the same time Lord Northcliffe was named Director of Propaganda in Enemy Countries, and Directors were appointed for neutral countries for intelligence, and for cinematograph propaganda. Lord Northcliffe was technically responsible to Lord Beaverbrook in respect of finance, but, in fact, he had the right of direct access to the Prime

[1] 66 *H. C. Deb*, 5s., col. 549, 9 September, 1914.

Minister and the War Cabinet. Confusion was worse con-
founded by locating the Enemy Propaganda Department in
the British War Mission with which Northcliffe had been
working for some months past. Informal conferences were
inaugurated to co-ordinate efforts, and later a Propaganda
Policy Committee was presided over by Lord Northcliffe.
A working unity was actually achieved, although at the
expense of many weary months and years of bickering and
duplication.[1] The Italians arrived at this same method of
organization.

The most important difference between the American and
the British plan was that the latter put foreign and domestic
propaganda in the hands of co-ordinate officials. When the
technicalities of the matter are allowed for, the British system clearly made no distinction between Northcliffe and
Beaverbrook, for instance, who both had direct access to the
Prime Minister and the War Cabinet. The British, in
effect, laid equal emphasis upon the necessity for depart-
mental autonomy in dealing with home, empire, neutral,
allied, and enemy propaganda. The extraordinary diver-
sity of foreign interests to which the British were appealing
probably justified this procedure, because the problems
which were presented were highly distinct.[2] The Americans

---

[1] The attitude of the Foreign Office clique toward the Beaverbrook
ministry is reflected in the comments of the anonymous author of *The
Pomp of Power*. He says that a group of experts on foreign affairs refused
to work under the direction of Beaverbrook and migrated to the Foreign
Office. Beaverbrook relied upon Canadians " whose experience of foreign
affairs and whose knowledge of foreign languages was as limited as his
own." Beaverbrook has told his own story in *Politicians and the Press*.
Lord Bertie, British Ambassador to France, lamented that for two years
(until 1917) the Foreign Office failed to establish a Press bureau in Paris.
(*Diary*, 1914-18, II : 203.)

[2] This will appear especially in connection with a later point.

came into the War, when it was neither their business to win the neutrals, nor to play one group against another. They had a very simple propaganda message to get across (American preparations ; a Wilsonian Peace), and it could be vested in one executive without much danger.

It was the Germans who had a minimum of co-ordinated propaganda effort.   Each Department went ahead in its own way, and the only formal co-operation was in the Press conference, which met two or three times a week.   The War Ministry, the General Staff, the Navy Department, the District Military Authorities, the Colonial Office, the Post Office, the Interior Department, the Treasury Department, the Food Ministry, and eventually, the Foreign Office took part.   The chairmanship was passed round in a rotating system, and the co-operating journalists chose a committee to speak for them.

The Military Authorities had to build their work from the ground up.[1]   At the outbreak of the War there was but a single official who had contact with the Press.   But they soon evolved an extensive Press service to report military operations, to edit the Field Press, to control the admission of home papers to the army, and to carry on propaganda against the enemy.

The Foreign Office was slow in clearing for action, but in October, 1914, when the check on the Marne had deferred the prospects for peace, a special *Zentralstelle für Auslands-*

---

[1] Nicolai complains that the Reichstag failed to vote them enough money to develop a satisfactory Press section before the war, because " in peace times the Press was conceived as a partisan instrument." Nicolai, *Nachrichtendienst, Presse u. Volksstimmung,* p. 53.

dienst was created. This was a very busy bureau and published an imposing array of propaganda material.

As the War developed, the conflict between military and civil authorities became more and more acute. The military men went into a paroxysm of rage when the peace resolution was moved by Erzberger in 1917, as they had when Bethmann-Hollweg held out the olive branch in 1916. The military authorities had no patience with palaver about peace ; they wanted a victorious peace of dictation. Ludendorff granted an interview to the Berlin Press in which these views were put before the people. Instantly the Left and Centre took up the challenge, and assailed the military for trying to interfere in politics. The Chancellor, to avoid being caught between partisan fires, refused, as had his predecessor, to create a separate Minister of Propaganda. The military authorities had proposed this on three different occasions, for they had already begun to feel the effects of Allied propaganda. At last the G.H.Q. tried to reach the home public directly by establishing a special Press service called the *Deutsche Kriegsnachrichten*, which, in spite of the opposition of the large papers, prospered. At the direction of General Ludendorff an elaborate plan of patriotic stimulation was drawn up. It was designed to reach the civilian and the fighting population.[1]

There were other tentative gestures toward the formation of a special propaganda agency to co-ordinate German efforts at home and abroad, but all of them failed. Private citizens organized the Wagner Culture Committee, to spread pro-German propaganda very early in the War, but its work

[1] The memorandum of July 29, 1927, is printed in Nicolai, p. 119 ff.

lacked both prestige and deftness. Germany suffered from the overzealous efforts of private persons to fill the gaps left by Government omissions. Professor Lamprecht spoke with contempt of the educated man who " obtained the largest possible goose quill, and wrote to all his foreign friends, telling them that they did not realize what splendid fellows the Germans were, and not infrequently adding that, in many cases, their conduct required some excuses. . . . The consequences were gruesome." In 1916, some of the civilian authorities commended the movement to form a *Deutscher National-Ausschuss*, but this was still a private venture. Chancellor Hertling at last took some steps toward unified control in August, 1918, but his measures were both inadequate and tardy.

The French kept their propaganda in the hands of the established diplomatic, military and naval agencies. Occasionally they supplemented the work abroad by sending out a High Commissioner, who combined propaganda, economic and other functions, as did the temporary war missions of all the allied powers. The *Maison de la Presse* had its agents attached to the legations abroad.[1]

When Allies are fighting together, the problem of co-ordinating their propagandas and their policies arises. Inter-Allied co-operation in the last War was in a rudimentary stage at the time of the Armistice. When Lord Northcliffe became head of the British Enemy Propaganda Department in February, 1918, he called a preliminary

[1] A committee to conduct artistic propaganda abroad was formed in the spring of 1918 under the direction of the Minister for Education and Fine Arts. Besides the *Maison de la Presse* there were unofficial members from organizations like the *Chambre syndicale de la haute couture. Journal Officiel*, 8th March, 1918.

conference on inter-Allied propaganda. One of the participating experts, Mr. Wickham Steed of *The Times*, writes that M. Henri Moysset, chief private secretary to the French Minister of Marine, spoke as a French representative, and insisted upon the imperative necessity for creating a " Thinking General Staff " to unify the effort exerted by the Allies in enemy and neutral countries. The Conference did actually appoint Professor Borghese (Italy), Mr. Steed and M. Moysset, with the expectation that they would co-operate in Paris, but jealousy of Moysset is said to have prevented the full development of the work.[1] The Allies conducted a formal conference in August, 1918, and their most successful common venture was a Permanent Inter-Allied Commission at the Italian G.H.Q.

Although the problem of organizing international propaganda campaigns was not satisfactorily solved in the late War, the experience of the Allies in certain other projects was complete enough to reveal sound principles of administration. Sir Arthur Salter, who digested his experience with the Inter-Allied Shipping Control with such skill, has generalized the conditions of continuing co-operation upon executive matters between independent governments.

> Contact, and indeed regular contact, must be established between the appropriate permanent officials of the several national administrations. It is important that these officials should (where possible) continue to exercise executive authority in their own departments and, where geographical reasons prevent this, that they should, at least, be specialists, and continue to exercise a decisive influence on them. The officials must enjoy the confidence of the respective ministers, must keep in constant touch

[1] Steed, *Through Thirty Years*, II : 196.

with their policy, must, within a considerable range, be able to influence their action, and they must have an accurate knowledge of the limits of their own influence.[1]

He declares that they must work together in sufficient intimacy to develop trust or knowledge of the limits within which they may trust one another, and that they must endeavour to develop such relations as will enable them, without disloyalty to their own governments, to discuss policy frankly in the earlier stages before it has been formulated in their own countries. The formal authority may best be supplied by the occasional meeting of the responsible ministers. Formal meetings of international representatives ought to be solely for the purpose of ratifying agreements already arrived at informally. Even minor negotiation should never be in the nature of a bargain.

Salter argues that the arrangement which he suggests, is an appropriate solution of the rôle of committees in administration.

> Nothing is so ineffective as a committee which consists of persons, each of whom has no specialized function and no personal executive authority, and yet tries to direct executive action. But if a number of persons, each of whom has a direct executive authority, which he continues to exercise in his own special sphere, meet from time to time, in order to dovetail their common measures and adjust them to a common plan, and then return to their departments to put into effect what they have agreed the committee is an effective instrument of co-operative action.

Assuming that the problem of co-ordinating inter-ally propagandas can be satisfactorily disposed of, our attention

[1] J. A. Salter, *Inter-Allied Shipping Control*, p. 257.

may revert to the problem of domestic organization. Once agreed that unity should be attained, the issue then arises as to whether the propaganda organization should seek to work through the existing diplomatic machinery abroad, or whether it should assemble separate staffs for that type of propaganda work. The late War seemed to show that special *ad hoc* agencies should be established abroad, even though the diplomatic staffs were often resentful of their new colleagues in the foreign field. Mrs. Vira B. Whitehouse, for instance, was sent to Switzerland by the Committee on Public Information. The Legation met her cordially, but, owing to the vagueness with which her instructions were defined, refused to give her the recognition and the facilities which were indispensable to her work. It was only after a special trip to Washington that a long and vexatious campaign of polite sabotage was surmounted.[1]

The diplomatic service is less likely to possess the type of personnel necessary to cope with a new and experimental service, such as propaganda, than an agency whose staff is explicitly recruited for the purpose. In some cases, too, the gum shoe tradition is detrimental to efficiency. The tactics of the American Committee on Public Information, which explained its purpose to the neutral government in whose territory it wished to operate, shocked many diplomats, who were trained in stealthiness.

What about the personnel of the propaganda service? The director of each major branch ought to be a man whose prestige equals that of the policy-determining officials. Now policy and propaganda should work together, hand and

[1] *A Year as a Government Agent* tells the story.

glove.   General Ludendorff, whose astute observations on propaganda have won general recognition, has written that " Good propaganda must keep well ahead of actual political events.   It must act as a pace-maker to policy and mould public opinion, without appearing to do so." [1]   The worst thing possible is for the propagandists and the diplomats to contradict one another openly.   As a member of the House of Commons declared in discussing the problem : " Nothing can be more serious than a double voice in our Foreign Affairs." [2]

It is important to give the propagandist a place, not only in the actual execution of policy, but in the formation. Policies are not safely formulated without expert information on the state of that opinion upon which they rely for success. Those who are occupied with propaganda live under circumstances in which the daily balancing and weighing of delicate currents of public sentiment is their job.   Now the full import of estimates of the state of public opinion cannot be realized unless they are urged by personalities whose prestige is at least the equal of those who have the deciding hand in matters of policy.   It is not necessary that the heads of the propaganda services should formally occupy ministerial or cabinet posts, but they should have ministerial or cabinet influence, in fact.

This, I submit, is a legitimate inference from the rôle which Lord Northcliffe played in Great Britain.   When he took over the Enemy Propaganda work, he quickly became aware of the crucial importance of forcing a decision upon

[1] See *Meine Kriegserinnerungen*, pp. 284–313.
[2] 109 *H. C. Deb*, 5s., col. 987.

certain hitherto uncertain and contradictory questions of policy. The British Government had joined others in making contradictory promises to the Italians, and to the South Slavs, and it was high time for the obscurity to be dispelled. He demanded prompt action by the Cabinet, and was so successful that the scruples of Downing Street and of Italy were swept aside in time for a great propaganda offensive, to be launched against the Austro-Hungarian troops, which had the effect of forcing the postponement of the Piave offensive.

The offensive was timed for April, 1918, and, according to Wickham Steed and Sir Campbell Stuart it was postponed until the end of June, because of the demoralizing inroads of Allied propaganda on the Southern Slav regiments.

In the United States it was of no particular importance that Mr. Creel lacked prestige. The foreign policy of the country was made by President Wilson, and it happened to have great propaganda value.

Is it desirable for the leaders of propaganda to be recruited from among the most powerful newspaper proprietors and editors ? The selection of such a man is certain to arouse nasty insinuations in the legislature. After the announcement that a number of editors and proprietors had been appointed to posts in the British service, a member of the House rose to inquire :

Is it the intention of the Government to " nobble " every editor in London ? (The editors of the *Express*, *Times*, *Daily Mail*, *Evening Post*, *Chronicle* and certain other leading papers were involved.)

Mr. Austen Chamberlain put the criticism with less brevity and more wisdom.

> As long as you have the owner of a newspaper as a member of your Administration, you will be held responsible for what he writes in the newspapers. You would not allow a colleague, not the owner of a newspaper, to go down and make speeches contrary to the policy of His Majesty's Government, or to attack men who are seving His Majesty's Government. You cannot allow them, instead of making speeches, to write articles or to permit the articles to be written in their newspapers. My right hon. Friend and his Government will never stand clear in the estimation of the public, and will never have the authority which they ought to have, and which I desire them to have, until they make things quite clear, open and plain to all the world and sever this connection with the newspapers.[1]

The Prime Minister, Mr. Lloyd George, minimized the force of this objection by directing attention to the fact that :

> the rule which applies to all company directors and professional men joining the Government must be applicable also to newspapermen, and as soon as the two Ministers were appointed, they gave up all direction of their papers.[2]

To this, Mr. Chamberlain replied by denying that the analogy of a private company is applicable to the Press.

> If its independence is supposed to have been sacrificed by the acceptance of Ministerial obligations, then the Press loses its freedom, and with its freedom loses its authority.

He deplored certain unfortunate coincidences. After an attack in the Press upon certain ministerial colleagues :

> the Government finds it impossible, thereafter, to retain in office the officials who are specially attacked, and the

[1] 103 *H. C. Deb,* 5s., col. 657.   [2] 104 *H. C. Deb.,* 5s., col. 40.

people who are specially associated with those attacks . . .
are shortly thereafter found, in this case, on their
individual merits, and that alone, to be indispensable to
the Government in particular offices.[1]

Mr. Lloyd George replied to these insinuations by saying
that he knew there would be a row about these appointments,
and that he was right, but that he had found that only
newspapermen could really do the job.

It is true that newspapermen are the most desirable, but
it is not, therefore, necessary to choose one of the biggest
owners and editors. If a less conspicuous man is selected,
he is, however, liable to snubs, as a mere second-rater.
England chose her Hearst to conduct propaganda against
the enemy ; the United States chose a man of tremendous
energy, but little reputation. Any proprietor who has had
sufficient strength to make his mark has undoubtedly
contracted enough animosities to impair his usefulness, and
the same thing is true of a journalist or editor. The sticking
point is the one to which Mr. Chamberlain referred, and the
humbler journalist is free from objection on this count. It
would, therefore, seem that the balance of the scale on
this particular matter inclines toward the American
practice.

There is no doubt about the superlative qualifications of
newspapermen for propaganda work. The stars in the
propaganda firmament during the world war were mostly
journalists, though there were a few literary men, like H.G.
Wells, and widely travelled and alert historians, like Seton-
Watson. And the journalists who delivered the goods were

[1] 104 *H. C. Deb.*, 5s., col. 76.

not, primarily, the editorial writers. They were men, whose primary business was reporting or editing the news. Northcliffe was essentially a reporter, and Steed had spent long years in the foreign service of *The Times.*

Newspapermen win their 'daily bread by telling their tales in terse, vivid style. They know how to get over to the average man in the street, and to exploit his vocabulary, prejudices and enthusiasms. As Mr. Spencer Hughes remarked in the House of Commons, they are not hampered by what Dr. Johnson has termed " needless scrupulosity." They have a feeling for words and moods, and they know that the public is not convinced by logic, but seduced by stories.

What not to do has been nowhere better illustrated than in Germany. The Prussian officer who had charge of the propaganda work for the General Staff was a most sincere and conscientious gentleman. He had, however, a singular unfitness for his job, as this story will show. An American newspaperman in Berlin had known him for some time. Shortly after the Allies had created a tremendous uproar about the execution of Nurse Cavell, the French executed two German nurses under substantially the same circumstances. Not a murmur in the German Press. The American saw the official shortly afterwards and asked—

> Why don't you do something to counteract the British propaganda in America ?
> Why, what do you mean ?
> Raise the devil about those nurses the French shot the other day.
> What ? Protest ? The French had a perfect right to shoot them !

Which, of course, was probably true, but utterly irrelevant to propaganda. A Prussian officer simply could not look at the situation with the naïve indignation of an untutored civilian. But it was civilians whose opinions were ultimately deciding.

Propaganda personnel ought to be recruited from among those who possess intimate knowledge of the group to which they are supposed to appeal. " Hansi," whose real name was Waitz, was an Alsace-Lorrainer, who had fled to France in the Summer of 1914, to escape punishment at the hands of the German authorities for his seditious propaganda. He organized the French propaganda against the Germans, and his beautiful and highly idiomatic German was buttressed by a complete knowledge of local allusions. He very properly lays it down that propaganda should be well written for whatever audience it is intended.

Bismarck's sense of the important led him to take infinite pains in matters of style. Busch, his propaganda secretary, tells about an article which he read over to Bismarck.

> It was to be dated from Paris, and published in the *Kölnische Zeitung*. He said, " Yes, you have correctly expressed my meaning. The composition is good, both as regards its reasoning and the facts which it contains. But no Frenchman thinks in such a logical and well-ordered fashion, yet the letter is understood to be written by a Frenchman. It must contain more gossip, and you must pass more lightly from point to point. A Parisian Liberal writes the letter and gives his opinion as to the position of his party toward the German question, expressing himself in the manner usual in statements of that kind."[1]

[1] Busch, *Bismarck*, I : 8.

Within recent years there has been a development which may transform the personnel question in the future. Propaganda has become a profession. The modern world is busy developing a corps of men who do nothing but study the ways and means of changing minds or binding minds to their convictions. Propaganda, as remarked in the opening pages of this study, is developing its practitioners, its professors, its teachers and its theories. It is to be expected that governments will rely increasingly upon the professional propagandists for advice and aid.

Yet another question of propaganda organization is the problem of co-ordinating the efforts of central and local branches of the service. Ambassador Bernstorff complains of the inadequacy of the material sent to America by the German in Berlin,

> the Press-service (German) never succeeded in adapting itself to American requirements. The same may be said of most of the German propaganda which reached America in fairly large quantities since the third month of the War, partly in German and partly in not always irreproachable English. This, like the Press telegrams, showed a complete lack of understanding of American national psychology. The American character, I should like to repeat, is by no means so dry and calculating as the German picture of an American business man usually represents. The outstanding characteristic of the average American is rather a great, even though superficial, sentimentality. There is no news for which a way cannot be guaranteed through the whole country, if clothed in a sentimental form. Our enemies have exploited this circumstance with the greatest refinement, in the case of the German invasion of " poor little Belgium," the shooting of the " heroic nurse," Edith Cavell, and other incidents. Those who had charge of the Berlin propaganda, on the other hand, made very little of such occurrences on the enemy side, *e.g.*, the violation of

Greece, the bombing of Corpus Christi procession in Karlsruhe, etc. One thing that would have exerted a tremendous influence in America, if its publicity had been handled with only average skill, was the suffering of our children, women and old people, as a result of the British hunger blockade—that they have made no attempt to bring to the notice of the world.[1]

He also complains that Berlin sent arguments instead of news.

Here was the opinion of the man on the spot. He felt that the men at the centre were messing their job. His own anxiety to take advantage of what he calls the " sentimentality " of the American mind, led him to encourage a movement which was ultimately ruined because the central authorities failed to support it. Bernstorff tells the story thus :

Since the *Lusitania* catastrophe I had adopted the principle, and put it into practice as far as possible, of leaving the propaganda to our American friends, who were in a position to get an earlier hearing than we, and in any case understood the psychology of the Americans better than the Imperial German agents. Indeed, the words " German propagandist " had already become a term of abuse in America . . . a " Citizen's Committee for Food Shipments " was formed, whose activities spread through the whole country and were avowedly pro-German. A special function of the committee of Dr. von Mach as executive chief was a month of propaganda throughout the country with the object of obtaining the means to supply the children of Germany with milk. The English control of the post even led to the bold plan of building a submarine, to run the milk through the English blockade. The propaganda was very vigorously attacked by the greater part of the American Press, but pursued its course unafraid, collected money, submitted protests to the State Department against the attitude of the Entente, and so on.

[1] *My Three Years in America*, p. 53.

Dr. von Mach succeeded in bringing the matter to the notice of the President, who actively interested himself in it, and promised to see that the milk should pass the English blockade and reach Germany in safety. Accordingly, the State Department instructed the American Embassy in Berlin to issue a statement. Meanwhile, the well-known American journalist, McClure, returned from a tour of investigation in Germany, where he had been supported in every way by the German Government Departments. He gave a very favourable account of the milk question, as of the feeding of infants in general, and this gave rise to the first disagreeable controversy. McClure took up an unyielding attitude. Unfortunately, however, the State Department then published an equally favourable report, which, coming from the American Embassy and published with the approval of the Foreign Office in Berlin, caused the complete collapse of Dr. von Mach. This incident made a most painful impression in America, and led to a series of bitter attacks on Dr. von Mach and the whole movement, which was thus exposed in a most unfortunate light. The favourable report on the milk question was drawn up by a Dr. E. A. Taylor, and definitely confirmed and, indeed, inspired by the German authorities.[1]

The Ambassador related this incident to discredit the central authorities, but perhaps greater responsibility rested on him for pursuing a policy which he had reason to know was distasteful to those authorities. And in this case the better reason seems to be on the side of Berlin, for they knew that to advertise a milk shortage would be to encourage the tenacious fighting spirit of the Allies and, in particular, to tighten the economic boycott of Germany. The man on the spot, Bernstorff, knew the value of a sentimental appeal, and he was right in this ; but he was unwilling to bend his

[1] Bernstorff, p. 259.

judgment to that of the central authorities and to refrain from encouraging a certain type of propaganda, which was likely to produce more harm than good. This incident illustrates the necessity for harmonious relations between the men at the centre and the men at the circumference, for Bernstorff was right in some particulars, and the central authorities were right in others. In most cases, Bernstorff was better advised than Berlin. Harmonious relations depend upon congenial personnel and can be but slightly affected by the mechanisms of organization.

While the discussion of propaganda organization had thus far dwelt upon problems of administration, there is no question of organization of more interest to the student of political science than the proper relation between legislative control and propaganda departments..

Propaganda is likely to be abused to promote personal and partisan ends, and the line of distinction between a private advantage which is incidental to a legitimate public advantage, and a private advantage which brings no overwhelming public advantage, is difficult to draw. A member of the British Parliament once called attention to a laudatory illustrated biography of the Prime Minister which was being circulated at public expense as part of British war propaganda.[1] Of course, it could be said that confidence in the Prime Minister was peculiarly necessary to war moral, and that such an expenditure was fitting and proper. It could also be said that the tone of the book was too full of adulation to free it from partisan suspicion.

Mr. Creel once put his foot in it by thanking God that

[1] 109 *H. C. Deb.*, 5s., col. 978.

the United States had been unprepared for war. To the Republicans this seemed to be the baldest possible attempt to whitewash the Democratic administration, and a fiery controversy broke out on the floor of Congress. Mr. Rainey came to the aid of the besieged head of the Committee on Public Information, by reminding the House that the Republicans had possessed power for sixteen consecutive years, right down to the two years before the European War, and if the Chairman had returned thanks for unpreparedness, he was returning thanks for the Republicans even more than for the Democrats.[1]

Sometimes it appears to be in the public interest, for current facts to be suppressed, but this is liable to the gravest abuse, for it is also to the interest of those in power, to suppress facts, in order to avoid criticism. Legislative bodies look with a suspicious eye upon any evidence of partisan concealment. During a time when the American aviation programme was an object of uneasy attention, certain aeroplane photographs were released by the Committee on Public Information with sub-titles of this nature : " Though hundreds have already been shipped, our factories have reached quantity production, and thousands upon thousands will soon follow." It was obvious that, if news of this character was circulated among the American people, the public would look with impatience upon the opposition Senators who were condemning the Administration for the inadequacy of its aviation policy.[2] The Republicans in the Senate turned their heavy artillery on

---

[1] *U.S. Cong. Rec.*, 65th Cong., 2nd Sess., p. 4859.
[2] *U.S. Cong. Rec.*, 65th Cong., 2nd Sess., pp. 4254 ff.

the Committee. The Committee claimed to have based its optimism upon authorized information from the aeroplane authorities. This appeared to be the truth, but there was no doubt that the report conveyed an exaggerated idea to the public.

In another case there was good *prima facie* evid nce for suspecting that the Naval authorities had used the Committee to mislead the public. On the fourth of July, 1917, the public was congratulated upon the fact that our transports had arrived on the other side, although " twice attacked by German submarines." A correspondent of the Associated Press, who was reported to have been aboard the transports, sent back a story to the effect that the sea had been smooth, and the voyage uneventful. Even such administration organs as the *New York Times* joined in the demand for an explanation. The Republicans launched into a terrific tirade against the Committee, the Navy Department and the whole Administration. It eventually appeared that the transports had gone over in four divisions, and that two of them had encountered no trouble, but that two had encountered submarines.[1] Here was a case in which public sentiment was genuinely disturbed by an apparent fabrication, and Congress did right in ventilating its suspicions. But it did so in an insulting manner, which was well calculated to diminish public confidence in the integrity and competence of those responsible for conducting the War.

As Winston Churchill has agreed, the reasons " certainly had weight "[2] which moved the censorship to discourage or

---

[1] *U.S. Cong. Rec.*, 65th Cong., 1st Sess., pp. 4811 ff.
[2] Winston Churchill, *The World Crisis*, 1916-18, I : 12.

forbid the "writing up" of any general other than the Commander-in-Chief in France and Britain. But the unavoidable result was to entrench the Commander-in-Chief in public esteem when good reason existed for removing him. The general public in Britain banked upon Kitchener long after the better informed were aware of the shortcomings of "Lord K of Chaos." The French people relied upon Joffre long after the experts began to take his stolidity for stupidity and his equanimity for insensitivity. Legislatures and cabinets were highly taxed, in inventing adroit means of kicking these leaders upstairs, and clearing the road for more capable chiefs. They had to reconcile the diverging claims of competence and public confidence.

Still another danger of abusing propaganda agencies lies in the possibility that public propaganda may be misused for commercial and class purposes. An attack upon the British Ministry of Information was made in Parliament by Mr. Leif Jones, who pointed to suspicious circumstances. First he gave the business connections of the most prominent men in the Ministry :

> Lord Beaverbrook . . . is a director of seven companies (was said to have withdrawn from active control). . . . Mr. Snagge is Secretary to the Ministry. He is a director of nine companies, and chiefly interested in rubber. The Director of Information in Scandinavia and Spain is Mr. Hambro, a member of the House, a banker, a railway director. . . . Take the Director of Propaganda for Switzerland—Mr. Guinness, who is director of nine companies. . . . Colonel Bryan, who assists in American propaganda, is director of six companies, mainly interested in ships and ship-building. Colonel Galloway, Assistant Director of Hospitality, is a director of five or six companies. . . . Mr. Cunliffe Owen is a director of thirty-six companies. I

understand they are all tentacles of a great tobacco trust, of which Mr. Cunliffe Owen is vice-chairman. This gentleman is placed in charge of propaganda throughout Asia and the Far East, including Japan.

He then proceeded to the point of his remarks :

> I have a record of a very extraordinary film which is being performed now. . . . The title of the picture was " Once a Hun, always a Hun." It first of all depicts two German soldiers in a ruined town in France. They meet a woman with a baby in her arms, and strike her to the ground. The two German soldiers then gradually merge into two commercial travellers, and are seen in an English village after the war. One of the travellers enters a small village general store, and proceeds to show to the shopkeeper a pan. The shopkeeper at the beginning is somewhat impressed by what is offered him for sale, when his wife comes in and, turning the pan upside down, sees marked on it " Made in Germany." She then indulges in a good deal of scorn at the expense of the commercial traveller and calls in a policeman, who orders the German out of the shop. A final notice, flashed on the screen, was to the effect that there cannot possibly be any more trading with these people after the war, and under this statement were the words, " Ministry of Information." The question of the policy of trade after the war has got to be decided by this country, but I hope the Ministry of Information does not intend to decide it before we have an opportunity even of discussing the Government policy.[1]

The attack was much more than a bare insinuation that capitalistic interests had suborned national propaganda. It alleges that the Ministry of Information was committing the country in advance to a policy which the legislature had not yet decided upon. The famous pronouncement by Lord Northcliffe at the end of the War had something of

[1] 109 *H. C. Deb.*, 5s., cols. 95 5ff.

the same significance. Northcliffe was a member of a committee appointed by the British Cabinet to develop a formula of peace terms (war aims). He met with the representatives of the War Cabinet, the Admiralty, the War Office, the War Aims Committee, and the Official Press Bureau. The agreed formula was first given out by Lord Northcliffe in an address before the United States' officers in London, on October 22nd, 1918. On the 4th of November they were published in *The Times* under the title " From War to Peace," from whence they were reproduced around the world.

It is always possible that propaganda will prejudice the position of a minority group in the community. The Irish members of Parliament protested against the Ministry on account of some aspects of its American propaganda. Mr. Devlin declared,

> One of the books, which has been published in America, is called " The Oppressed English," written by Ian Hay. This is a book, paid for by the Ministry of Information. . . . Although it has been sent all round America, it has not been allowed in this country. (It is) a tissue of falsehoods from beginning to end.[1]

Since propaganda agencies on a large scale were novelties of the last war in democratic countries, the legislative control of their expenditures was poorly organized at first. The funds for British propaganda were mostly taken from the general vote of supply for " His Majesty's Foreign and other Secret Services." The Creel Bureau was at first constituted by Executive Order and financed from the $100,000,000

---

[1] 109 *H. C. Deb.*, 5s., col. 1029.

appropriation granted to the President for the general promotion of the defence of the country. When the abuse of the Creel Bureau reached the peak of insinuation and distrust, Mr. Creel decided to force an investigation by the Appropriations Committee, by applying to Congress for a specific appropriation. After a hearing, which consumed three days, the Committee endorsed an appropriation for a million and a quarter dollars, and commended the past record of the bureau.[1] In the future it will probably be possible to provide for propaganda work by direct appropriation from the beginning.

The legislatures discussed the details of propaganda administration rather freely during the last War. Mr. T. P. O'Connor was anxious to remove the vexatious system of censorship, which had been introduced at the outbreak of the War, and which had aroused so much opposition from American newspapermen. In September of 1914 he declared,

> There is no public opinion in the world which ought to be so well informed with regard to the causes of the War, or the incidents of this War, or the principles of this War, as the opinion of the United States of America.[2]

Complaints were often made that the British propaganda was lagging behind the German propaganda in neutral countries.

Congress was far from reticent in criticizing the work of the Committee on Public Information. Senator Lodge uttered a solemn warning against German peace propaganda,

[1] *H. Doc.*, No. 1168, 65th Cong., 2nd Sess. ; *U.S. Cong. Rec.*, 65th Cong., 2nd Sess., pp. 7910 ff.
[2] 66 *H. C. Deb.*, 5s., col. 759.

and attacked a book entitled *Two Thousand Questions and
Answers about the War,* which had been issued by the Committee with an Introduction by Mr. Creel. An officer
of the National Security League had characterized it as
a " masterpiece of German propaganda," and Mr. Lodge
called to it the attention of the Senate. The defence
given by Mr. Creel was-that he had written the preface without reading the book, which he received from Mr. Albert
Shaw, who in turn had come into the possession of the
manuscript from an Englishman of undoubted integrity ;
that he had become uneasy about the document when his
attention had been called to certain passages, and was
revising it.[1]

On another occasion, Senator Poindexter, who had acted
as something of an atrocity hound during the War, accused
the Committee of defending the Germans because a statement
had been issued under its authority denouncing the story
of an American sergeant, who had been crucified by the
Germans.[2] Senator Lenroot, of Wisconsin, defended the
Administration, saying :

> there was a general inference drawn that that (crucifixion
> and similiar atrocities) was a general practice. If it was
> not true, I think it is the duty of the War Department to
> deny it. The parents of these boys are suffering agonies
> enough now, without being led to believe that unspeakable
> outrages are being committed upon all of our American
> soldiers who may be captured.

The legislative proceedings are full of attacks upon the
personnel of the propaganda services. The tenor of much

[1]   *U.S. Cong. Rec.,* 65th Cong., 2nd Sess., pp. 1037 ff.
[2]   Same, pp. 9056 ff.

of this criticism may be gathered by perusing these Congressional remarks upon Mr. Creel :

> Mr. Penrose (Senator from Pennsylvania). I do not see why we should permit men like Mr. Creel, for instance, whose scurrilous and defamatory utterances on the Constitution of the United States were read in this body the other day, to be holding an office and publishing a publicity chronicle, when he is smeared all over with treason.[1]
>
> Mr. Longworth (Representative from Ohio). Mr. Speaker, if I have any apologies to make to this House or anybody for the opinion that I enunciated about this man who, the day before yesterday, insulted the patriotism of the American people, and to-day insults the American Congress, it is that my language was far too temperate (applause).[2]
>
> Mr. Sherman (Senator from Illinois). Congress is stigmatized as a slum by a public officer created by an Executive Order, and paid by an appropriation made by the body he traduces. . . . After this, any servile deputy candle-snuffer is at liberty to revile us at pleasure. Any gangrened egotist afflicted with an ingrowing conceit may hereafter spurn Congress, and demand appropriations to feed him with the complacent assurance that precedent now justified everything.[3]

The immunities of Congress were used so recklessly that Mr. Creel was led to remark,

> The heavens may fall, the earth may be consumed, but the right of a Congressman to lie and defame remains inviolate.[4]

Lord Northcliffe and the others in England came in for the severest censure, but Parliament conducted itself with more restraint and dignity than Congress.

---

[1] *U.S. Cong. Rec.*, 65th Cong., 2nd Sess., p. 4827.
[2] Same, p. 4974. [3] Same, p. 8990.
[4] Creel, *How We Advertised America*, p. 52.

It is abundantly clear from this review of the relations between legislatures and propaganda bureaux that there is bound to be ample opportunity for misunderstanding, criticism and suspicion. Unless the legislature is informed and critical, the propaganda branches may be perverted to partisan, personal and class ends ; if the legislature is superfluously critical, the confidence of the public in its leaders may be destroyed, and moral impaired. It is humanly improbable that a satisfactory middle course can be steered, since this depends upon the voluntary restraint of the legislature. The only hope lies in confidential and informal relations between administrators and legislators, supplemented by an appeal to publicity when the legislator can justify such conduct to his own conscience. Personal explanations at the dinner table, the clubhouse, the lounge, or the street corner, are the lubricants of the great and complicated machinery of government.[1]

This completes our survey of the problem of organizing a war-time propaganda service to influence international attitudes. The succeeding chapters will outline the nature of the psychological appeals which appear to be necessary to accomplish the purpose of such a mechanism—the instigation of animosity toward the enemy, the preservation of friendship between allies and neutrals, and the demoralization of the enemy.

[1] The problem of arriving at a financial estimate of what may be accomplished by propaganda is broached in a succeeding chapter.

CHAPTER III

WAR GUILT AND WAR AIMS

So great are the psychological resistances to war in modern nations that every war must appear to be a war of defence against a menacing, murderous aggressor. There must be no ambiguity about whom the public is to hate. The war must not be due to a world system of conducting international affairs, nor to the stupidity or malevolence of all governing classes, but to the rapacity of the enemy. Guilt and guilelessness must be assessed geographically, and all the guilt must be on the other side of the frontier. If the propagandist is to mobilize the hate of the people, he must see to it that everything is circulated which establishes the sole responsibility of the enemy. Variations from this theme may be permitted under certain contingencies which we shall undertake to specify, but it must continue to be the leading *motif*.

The governments of Western Europe can never be perfectly certain that a class-conscious proletariat within the borders of their authority will rally to the clarion of war. Before 1914 the growth of the Social Democrats in Germany, the vogue of anti-patriotism in France, and the rising star of the labourers in England, filled the governing classes with foreboding. It was freely predicted that mobilization could be paralysed by a general strike, and that social revolution might raise its ominous head.

To the uncertainties of proletarian sentiment must be added the vagaries of conciliatory opinion. When the crisis of 1914 arose in Great Britain, it was at once evident that powerful elements in the Cabinet, the Liberal Party, the literary and even the financial world were opposed to intervention to aid France. The columns of the *Daily News*, a Left Wing Liberal organ, the *Manchester Guardian*, another Liberal paper, and the *Labour Leader* were flooded with letters, editorials and manifestos of protest against the idea of British participation in the impending struggle on the continent.

Let us remember, admonished the *Daily News* on the 29th day of July

> that the most effective work for peace that we can do is to make it clear that not a British life shall be sacrificed for the sake of Russian hegemony of the Slav world.

On the following day it wrote that the

> free peoples of France, England and Italy should refuse to be drawn into the circle of this dynastic struggle.

On the first of August, the *News* published a bitter protest against the policy of intervention, under the well-known initials, " A.G.G." The title was " Why we must not fight."

> For years under the industrious propaganda of Lord Northcliffe, Mr. Strachey, Mr. Maxse, and the militarists, this country has been preached into an anti-German frame of mind that takes no account of the facts. Where in the wide world do our interests clash with Germany ? Nowhere. With Russia we have potential conflicts over the whole of South-Eastern Europe and Southern Asia.

The Bishop of London, J. Ramsay MacDonald, Keir Hardie, Thomas Hardy, J. J. Thomson, Gilbert Murray, and scores of lesser celebrities protested against British aid to France and Russia on many different grounds. Most of these men were not proletarian internationalists, and they found reasons to object to war on grounds of the national interests of England. Most of them implied that war might, under some circumstances, be legitimate, but in the hour of decision they shrank from believing that the hour had come. Now, it is hard to conceive of an international complication in which divergent interpretations of national interest, nurtured by aversion to war and ruthlessness, will not precipitate dissent and controversy. The conciliatory frame of mind is prone to temporize and find good reason for delay.

Certain business and banking interests, when pulled up short by the prospect of imminent war, try to put on the brakes. That such international bankers as the Speyers and the Bonns were restraining influences during the first and second Moroccan crises is generally known. A less successful instance of such pressure upon those who wield political power is revealed by Wickham Steed, of the London *Times*. In the midst of the crisis in 1914 the financial editor of that paper, Mr. Hugh Chisholm, was urgently invited to call upon the head of one of the largest financial houses in the City. The financier told him flatly that the pro-war editorials in *The Times* must cease. They were hounding the country into war. The City of London was on the verge of a disaster, such as the world had never seen. Strict neutrality was the only course for England to adopt. He produced a message which he had just written to the head of the Paris house of his family, in which the alarming statement was made that the writer had only a billion pounds in the Bank of England and £800,000 in the Union of London and the Smith's Bank with which to meet engagements, and that the margin about obligations was so slight that the Paris house must refrain from drawing cheques or bills upon him. *The Times*, it may be added, did not succumb to this pressure, although certain members of the Cabinet were strongly moved by it.[1]

Every resource must be exploited if such inconvenient currents are to be turned aside. The identification of a particular foreign nation as the enemy may be established by three lines of inference. It invariably mobilizes first, in the days of crisis (either openly or secretly), and commits acts of war, and by doing so, reveals a criminal anxiety to press matters to a finish. More than that, it invariably incriminates itself by endeavouring to manœuvre our government into the position of an aggressor during the feverish negotiations preceding the final break. Behind all this, there invariably stands a record of lawlessness, violence and malice, which offers unassailable proof of a deliberate intent to maim or destroy us.

A typical bill of indictment is the one drawn up by *Le Petit Journal*, one of the " Big Five " of the Paris Press, on the 3rd of August. It gave its version of the war under the heading, " Machiavellian Duplicity." Germany secretly connived at the formulation of an unacceptable ultimatum to Serbia. She perfidiously protested her desire for peace. She tried to divide the Allies by urging France to apply the

[1] Steed, *Through Thirty Years*, II : 8.

pressure to Russia which she refused to apply to Austria. She tried to manœuvre France into the position of an aggressor in the eyes of England, by asking France to denounce the Alliance with Russia, or to declare her willingness to fight with Russia. Germany opened hostilities against France and violated French territory before she broke off diplomatic relations. She violated the neutrality of Belgium in the face of a solemn promise to protect it. In so doing, she was acting in complete harmony with her historical traditions of ruthless and barbarous dealing. Frederick the Great and the robbery of Maria Theresa are earnests of this.

These indictments come with peculiar weight from historians and from other men who are credited in the public mind with the single-minded pursuit of truth. German scholarship leaped to the colours in the last War in the famous and unforgettable manifesto, signed by ninety-three of her most illustrious intellectuals. Attached to the document were such names as Ehrlich, Behring, Röntgen, Ostwald, Harnack, Schmoller, Brentano, Nernst, Hauptmann, Sudermann, Eucken, Wundt, Eduard Meyer, Lamprecht, Wilamowitz, Humperdinck, Reinhardt and Liebermann. Serious historians and journalists combined to elucidate the responsibility of Germany's enemies in such co-operative ventures as *Zum geschichtlichen Verständnis des grossen Krieges* by A. O. Meyer, Graf Ernst Reventlow, R. Nebersberger, C. H. Becker, G. Küntzel and F. Meinecke (2 Aufl., Berlin, 1916). The forward policy of Russia in Europe, since her humiliation in the East at the hands of Japan, the lust for revenge in France, and the jealousy of Germany's expansion by England were the cardinal points in interpreting the War.   The immediate diplomacy of the conflict showed that Russia, secretly encouraged by France, had seized upon the Serbian complication to provoke a general war.   Russia had mobilized first, and had actually invaded German territory, as, indeed, had the French, before the severance of diplomatic relations.   The envious English, ostensibly neutral, but bound by secret understandings, had grasped their opportunity to crush the competitor, whose naval and commercial supremacy must be forestalled at all costs of morality and decency.

The crisis burst on France and Belgium with such paralysing suddenness and such devastating consequences, that there was little need for elaborate rationalizations about the instigator of the War.   The Germans had to explain the war in the West, because they were in foreign territory, and, therefore, prima facie the aggressor.   It was in Britain, with its territory intact and the issue of war or peace undetermined for many agonizing hours after the die was cast on the continent, where discussion and rationalization played an influential part.   Masterly appeals to the national interest, after the style of *The Times* on 31st July, were necessary to carry conviction to the more articulate elements of the community that Germany should be treated as an immediate and overwhelming menace.   It argued :

A German advance through Belgium to the north of France might enable Germany to acquire possession of Antwerp, Flushing, and even of Dunkirk and Calais, which might then become German naval bases against England. That is a contingency which no Englishman can look upon with indifference.   But if it is merely a contingency, why should England not wait until it is realized before acting or preparing to act ?   Because in these days of swift decision and swifter action, it would be too late for England to act with any degree of success after France had been defeated in the North. . . . Even should the German navy remain inactive, the occupation of Belgium and Northern France by German troops would strike a crushing blow at British security.   We should then be obliged alone and without Allies to bear the burden of keeping up a Fleet superior to that of Germany and of an army proportionately strong. This burden would be ruinous.

In the United States, where the issue of war or peace hung in the balance longer than in Great Britain, the disagreement over which group of belligerent powers was the enemy drew forth an unparalleled mass of rationalizations, suitable for circulation by the protagonists of either set.   The historians and the other seekers of the truth were no more reticent than their German colleagues in putting the blame on the enemy for the calamity of war, once war came.   The curious fact that in such emergencies the truth seekers find different truths, and that the differences are territorially segregated according to national boundaries, is once more exemplified in the Oxford War pamphlets, the Princeton symposium, or the Chicago war series, when they are placed side by side with the German literature alluded to above.   The facility with which sincere and dextrous hands may shape cases on either side of a controversy, leaves no doubt that, in the future, the propagandist may count upon a battalion of honest professors to rewrite history, to serve the exigencies of the moment, and to provide the material for him to scatter thither and yon.

There are, no doubt, profound psychological dispositions, which facilitate the work of the propagandist in fastening war guilt upon the technical enemy. Just what these tendencies are is a matter of obscurity and dispute, but perhaps the most ingenious explanation is the one put forward by Baschwitz, who describes the mind of the public as in conflict between the disagreeable fact of war and the wish to believe that the good is triumphant in the universe. It must, therefore, be that one's own nation is vindicating the right against the wrong.[1] Speculations of this sort are hazardous in the extreme, and the propagandist is content to accept the aid of his anonymous allies, while he busily multiplies the evidence of the responsibility of the enemy. He instigates or welcomes such a windfall as accrued to the cause of the Entente in the last War, when an eloquent volume, *J'accuse* (Lausanne, 1915), came from the pen of Richard Grelling, a native of Switzerland and close student of Germany. He bestirs himself to counter-attack against such telling thrusts, as did the Germans who brought Grelling's son, Kurt, to publish *Anti-J'accuse* at Zürich, in 1916. He scans the horizon for new material as the War evolves, as did the Germans when they scrutinized the captured Belgium archives for material, which might incriminate the Entente, and broadcasted everything which seemed to do so.

Now the task of the propagandist is just begun, when he fastens the guilt of willing the War upon an opposing nation. No sooner is the enemy located than the nation discharges its energies, churned in the crucible of hours and days of suspense, in instantaneous movements of defence and counter-attack. In the very act of delivering the blow the nation

[1] See Baschwitz, *Der Massenwahn*, passim.

calls for unity and victory. It is the business of the propagandist to amplify and repeat the call.

As early as the 29th of July, 1914, the London *Times* called upon all parties to " Close Ranks." The Kaiser united his people behind him, when he declared that he knew no party more. The Fascio came in Italy and the " *Union sacrée* " was proclaimed in the French Parliament. The sensational appeal of Gustave Hervé to the ranks of Labour was broadcasted far and wide. Hervé was a notorious *sans-patrie* who had belittled patriotism as an implement of capitalistic exploitation. On the very brink of the War he changed the name of his paper, *La Guerre Sociale*, into *La Victoire* and pleaded with all the ardour of his fervent spirit for unity :

> Amis socialistes, amis syndicalistes, amis anarchistes, qui n'êtes pas seulement l'avant-garde idéaliste de l'humanité ; mais qui êtes encore le nerf et la conscience de l'armée française, la patrie est en danger !
> La patrie de la Révolution est en danger ![1]

The call of the Empire—" Your King and Country calls you "—buried the hatchet in Ireland and brought recruits from all over the British dominions. The work of the Overseas League and the Victoria League in strengthening the ties of friendship and affection was vindicated. In order to illustrate the unity of the Empire, a number of profusely illustrated volumes were put out, showing the history of British beneficence and the degree of Empire co-operation at the front. There is *India and the War*, for example, edited with an introduction by Lord Sydenham

---

[1] *La Guerre Sociale*, July 31, 1914.

(1915), which glorifies British rule in India, and has page after page of coloured pictures, showing Indian regiments in native uniforms.

The call to unity is essentially a call to history, and the memory of a common past has powerful sentimental value. *La Libre Parole* for the second of August, 1914, thus admonished its readers :

> Haut les coeurs ! La France de Jeanne d'Arc, de Louis XIV et de Napoléon, la France de Bouvines, de Valmy, de Jéna, et de Montmirails n'a rien perdu de ses antiques vertus.

None of the sentiments which are deeply imbedded in the social tradition can afford to be neglected in justifying belligerent idealism through murder and hate. To the historical may be usually added the religious vocabulary. Never have these chords been strummed with greater dramatic sense than by Kaiser William II., as he looked over the surging throng in the Lustgarten on that epochal July night and said :

> A fateful hour has fallen for Germany.
> Envious peoples everywhere are compelling us to our just defence.
> The sword has been forced into our hands. I hope that if my efforts at the last hour do not succeed in bringing our opponents to see eye to eye with us and in maintaining peace, we shall with God's help so wield the sword that we shall return it to the sheath again with honour.
> War would demand of us enormous sacrifices of property and life, but we should show our enemies what it means to provoke Germany.
> And now I commend you to God. Go to church and kneel before God and pray for his help and for our gallant army.

Even such exuberance of sentiment as the Credo for France, prepared by M. Henri Lavedan, has its place :

> I believe in the courage of our soldiers and in the skill and devotion of our leaders. I believe in the power of right, and in the crusade of civilization, in France, the eternal, the imperishable, the essential. I believe in the reward of suffering and the worth of hope. I believe in confidence, in quiet thought, in the humble daily round, in discipline, in charity militant. I believe in the blood of wounds and the water of benediction ; in the blaze of artillery and the flame of the votive candle ; in the beads of the rosary. I believe in the hallowed vows of the old, and in the potent innocence of children. I believe in women's prayers, in the sleepless heroism of the wife, in the calm piety of the mother, in the purity of our cause, in the stainless glory of our flag. I believe in our great past, in our great present, and in our greater future. I believe in our countrymen, living and dead. I believe in the hands clenched for battle, and in the hands clasped for prayer. I believe in ourselves, I believe in God. I believe, I believe.[1]

This sort of verbal delirium is capable of very remarkable things, as when Albert de Mun, the venerable Catholic leader, solemnly implored God to " aid the sons of Clovis," alluding to one of the barbarous teutonic chieftains of early French history.[2] Graceful phrasemongers like Maurice Barres, who believed the spirit of France to be a " grave enthusiasm, a disciplined exaltation," can be trusted to furnish volatile words acceptable to less religious minds.

For the preponderating majority in any community the business of beating the enemy in the name of security and peace suffices. This is the great war aim, and in single-

---

[1] Translated in John Buchan, *History of the War*, Chapter XXII.
[2] *Le Gaulois*, August 5, 1914.

hearted devotion to its achievement they find that " peace-fulness of being at war," of which Principal Jacks once wrote.[1] In 1915, he glanced back over the first twelve months of the Great War, and observed that " the life of Great Britain has been acquiring a unitary aim of purpose. The aim itself is warlike ; but it has been attended with some increase of mental peace." He cast a jaundiced eye upon the pre-war world and wrote, " Regarded from the moral point of view, the scene was one of indescribable confusion. It was, in fact, a moral chaos. Our ' inner state,' in consequence, was marked by profound unrest." People were once uncertain of life, but now they had found a mission. The propagandist, indeed, can always count upon the state of mind which is here so gracefully expressed. Men with uncongenial spouses, wives with uncongenial husbands, youths with suppressed ambition, elderly men with their boredoms and faint yearnings for adventure, childless women and some wifeless men, the discredited ones who pine for a fresh deal in the game of life ; all, and many more, find peace from mental fight in the intoxication of life in one historical hour and for one historic goal.

This simple cry for unity and victory (with accompanying peace) is not enough. What form shall the victory take ? There are inquiring minds who push behind the formula of victory and seek to prescribe what shall be meant thereby. Indeed the whole function of war aims is to arouse ambition and to fortify the resolution of the community to overcome every resistance to fulfilment. The enemy must be made to appear as more than a menace to the social heritage ; the

[1] *New Republic*, September 11, 1915.

enemy is an obstacle to the realization of new national values. For the diplomatically-minded the war may become a war to expand the national influence in terms of lands and concessions and ports. This section of opinion in Germany gorged itself upon visions of a humiliated Britain, shorn of her fleet, and upon dreams of a partitioned France and Russia. In Britain the most popular war aim among these circles was the scrapping of the German Navy. For the French Victory meant the restoration of Alsace and Lorraine, and the partition of Germany.

But the propagandist must never permit himself to forget that in the complex communities of our time there are minds who find no peace in war. Graham Wallas testified not for himself alone, when he commented on Professor Jacks' article and said, " I should choose the unrest of thought because I desire that the war should come to an end the instant its continuance ceases to be the less of two monstrous evils, and because I believe that our national policy should, even during the fighting, be guided not only by the will to conquer, but also by the will to make possible a lasting peace."

Here is the mind for which war is a loathsome abomination, and which steadfastly refuses to believe that the defeat of a particular enemy is enough to make it worth getting on with. The primitive man, overtaken by catastrophe, hunts high and low for a scapegoat and a messiah. The scapegoat is the person who got him into the mess and the messiah is the person who will get him out. History is the story of the struggle of devils and deliverers. This primitive pattern of thought leads to the interpretation of war as the struggle between a good and a bad collective person.   Cleave to the good and punish the bad.   Such a formulation is by no means acceptable to the sophisticated few, who have come to believe that persons (individual or " collective ") act as they do, because of the tenacious grip of circumstances.   If things have gone badly in the past, the explanation is to be found in impersonal forces.   If it is hoped to produce better behaviour in the future, some fundamental forces must be adjusted.   It is no good wreaking vengeance for the past ; it is only profitable to take precautions for the future and to modify the conditions which have played havoc with the past.

The propagandist who deals with this new pattern of thought must be subtler than when he copes with the punitive pattern of mind.   If the adherents of the former are to join in condemning the enemy, it must be because they see in him the most powerful obstruction in the path toward the realization of new world conditions.   If their allegiance is to be won for the war, they must be furnished with war aims of a highly rationalized and idealistic type.

Propaganda of this sort played a decisive rôle in the late struggle for world supremacy, and the reasons are evident. If we examine the currents of public opinion in England during the weeks immediately preceding the crisis of 1914, we cannot fail to remark the numerous signs of specifically anti-war agitation.   In the London *Daily News* for the 15th of July an editorial was printed under the title, the " Octopus of Militarism," which declared the business of the armament makers to be

> cosmopólitan in its operations and soulless in its motives. It works upon the fears and hates of ignorant people, uses

the Press as the instrument of its purposes, and makes tools of the diplomats and statesmen, many of whom are financially interested in its success.

A few days later it addressed itself to the subject again, asking

> Why has the one (the duel) been abolished, and the other (war) left ? There is only one answer—that there is money in armaments and no money to speak of in duelling.

During the same weeks the new book by H. N. Brailsford, called *The War of Steel and Gold*, was running the gamut of the reviews. Polemic had not yet subsided over Norman Angell's thesis in *The Great Illusion*.[1] The quiet influence of John A. Hobson and of many other publicists in Liberal and Labour ranks helped to drive home the economic interpretation of war. Their writing was less tinctured by doctrinaire formulas than the corresponding work on the continent.

If anything, the socialists of France and Germany were more vociferous than the English in denouncing war and war-makers. But when the crucial moment came, the evidence of the culpability of the enemy was so overwhelming, that they joined the War. This decision split the Social Democrats in Germany, and left a discontented fraction in France, and as the War wore on, the discomforts of combat favoured the recovery of the old uncompromising attitude. The Socialist and Democratic papers in Germany became thorns in the side of the Imperial Government. A similar evolution went forward in France. Such Liberal

---

[1] See, incidentally, his forcible letter in the *Times* of August 1, 1914, against intervention.

elements as those associated with the personalities of Léon Bourgeois and Estournelles de Constant were allied to the workers in their very keen regret at the turn of affairs, and after the first shock of battle wore away, a certain recovery set in, much as it had in Germany.

While concessions were actually made to this type of sentiment in France and Germany, it was in England and in America that the most notice was taken of it. In both countries there was a period of hesitation before battle. H. G. Wells may be taken as an example of the pacifistically inclined Liberal, more gracefully articulate than most, whose support of the War came at the cost of inner struggle, and whose enthusiastic aid in a prolonged contest depended upon an elaborately rationalized cluster of war aims. Writing in the London *Daily Chronicle* for August 20th, 1914, he said :

> A war that will merely beat Germany a little and restore the hateful tension of the last forty years is not worth waging. As an end to all our efforts it will be almost an intolerable defeat. Yet unless a body of definite ideas is formed and promulgated now things may happen so.

Wells, of course, saw in " German militarism " one of the most colossal obstacles to the achievement of a better world order. His attitude of mind is precisely the one to be striven for by the inventor of war aims ; set up an ideal which will arouse the enthusiasm of those elements in the nation whose support is desired, and make it clear to them that the chief immediate stumbling block is the military enemy. This permits the scrupulous to kill with a clean conscience ; or, at least, to admonish the younger to do so.

When the Bolsheviki published the diplomatic correspondence which they found in the archives of the Tsar's government after the second revolution, a most embarrassing situation confronted the Allied Statesmen. For the Bolsheviki revealed for the first time to the world that the Allied governments had carved up large blocks of the world and raffled them off to one another. This raised some very disconcerting questions for those who had been talking about this War as different from every other war, since it was a war to end war and to make the world safe for democracy. By treaties signed in 1915, and subsequently, the possessions of the enemy powers were allotted to their future owners, without so much as a pretence at plebiscite or international control. In spite of the efforts of the Allied governments to suppress the knowledge of these incriminating documents in Great Britain, word soon reached the British labour leaders, and they bestirred themselves to force a show-down from the government. Mr. Lloyd George made a sensational speech on the fifth of January, 1918, in which he came out four-square for a peace acceptable to the conciliatory elements of the public. The secret history of this speech was not generally known until the publication of Woodrow Wilson's papers after the War. Among them is published a secret cablegram from Balfour, British Minister for Foreign Affairs, to the American State Department. Here is the despatch :

Following for information of the President, private and secret :—

Negotiations have been going on for some time between the Prime Minister and the Trade Unions. The main point was the desire of the Government to be released from certain pledges which were made to the Labour leaders earlier in the War.   This release is absolutely indispensable from the military point of view for the development of man power on the Western Front.   Finally the negotiations arrived at a point at which their successful issue depended mainly on the immediate publication by the British Government of a statement setting forth their war aims.   This statement has now been made by the Prime Minister.   It is the result of consultations with the Labour leaders as well as the leaders of the Parliamentary opposition.

Under these circumstances there was no time to consult the Allies as to the terms of the statement agreed upon by the Prime Minister and the above-mentioned persons. It will be found on examination to be in accordance with the declarations hitherto made by the President on this subject.

Should the President himself make a statement of his own views which in view of the appeal made to the peoples of the world by the Bolsheviki might appear a desirable course, the Prime Minister is confident that such a statement would also be in general accordance with the lines of the President's previous speeches, which in England as well as in other countries have been so warmly received by public opinion.   Such a further statement would naturally receive equally warm welcome.[1]

A point to be remembered by the working propagandist is that Liberal and middle-class people are likely to give their approval to war aims of a political or juristic character. The Labour ideology is more or less coloured by philosophies of economic determination which wound the property sentiment of the possessing classes.   If the problem of reconstructing the world is to be shorn of an apparent class bias, it must be conceived as a problem of a politico-juristic nature, for talk about world legislatures and courts tends to ingratiate itself where proposals for the administration

[1] R. S. Baker, *Woodrow Wilson and the World Settlement,* I : 40.

of raw materials by world action, and for the use of the world taxing power to level up existing inequalities of opportunity, are suspect. Phrases like " World Organization," " The United States of the Earth,"[1] " The Confederation of the World,"[2] " A World Union of Free Peoples," or " A League of Nations," slide trippingly from the tongue.

A war to vindicate international law thus has the sanction of bourgeois morality about it and avoids anything which tinges of a class issue. In the last War this idea figured heavily. Those who were arguing for British participation in the War, on grounds of national self-interest (vide *The Times*) chucked this article of faith out of the window, and transformed the War into a holy crusade for the Law of Nations when the news came that the Germans were marching into Belgium. The French organized a Committee for the Defence of International Law, headed by M. Louis Renault, of the Institute. The Germans were staggered by this outburst of affection for international law in the world, but soon found it possible to file a brief for the defendant. The cross-bill alleged that Belgium had not really been neutral, for the papers captured in her archives had revealed secret military conversations with the French and the British. The British, moreover, were reckless of the law of contraband and were invading the rights of neutrals on the high seas. The Germans, therefore, discovered that they were really fighting for the freedom of the seas and the rights of small nations to trade, as they saw fit, without being subject to

[1] See August Forel's pamphlet, *Die Vereinigten Staaten der Erde*, Bern u. Lausanne, 1914/15.
[2] See Louis Junod, *La confédération mondiale : Une alliance pour l'unification d. peuples*, Genève, 1914.

the bullying tactics of the British fleet. The Allies had already declared a war for the liberation of oppressed peoples, by which they understood at first no more than Belgium and Alsace and Lorraine. Later, the implications of this phrase were extended to cover the nationalities in the Austro-Hungarian Empire and the Poles in Germany. The Germans replied by saying that they, too, were fighting to liberate the oppressed, and, by this, they meant Ireland, Egypt and India.

A propagandist must always be alert to capture the holy phrase which crystallizes public aspiration about it, and under no circumstances permit the enemy to enjoy its exclusive use and wont. There are some holy phrases which have subversive connotations, unless they are promptly interpreted in a broad sense. When the members of the Union of Democratic Control in Great Britain began to say that they wanted the War to end secret diplomacy and to democratize foreign policy, they were talking about conditions in England as much as about conditions elsewhere. But the phrase was caught up by astute men, and turned into a criticism of the enemy.[1] It is the business of idealistic war aims to be invidious at the expense of the enemy.

Should there be a next general war, war aims of an idealistic character will probably be just as important as

---

[1] The Union of Democratic Control was organized in England by E. D. Morel, A. Ponsonby, and several others shortly after the outbreak of the War. It was instigated by indignation at the fact that the British Cabinet had secretly entered into engagements on the side of France which constituted in fact a commitment in advance to join in the War against a supposedly attacking Germany. It is interesting to note that the Bund Neues Vaterland, which was organized about the same time in Germany, spoke exactly the same language, and was quite unaware that the Union of Democratic Control in England was in existence.

they were in the last one.   International organizations are still
so weak that at least one other war could be fought on the
pretext of strengthening them.   Should the existing League
stigmatize any group of nations, there is no question that
this group would be the target of a very dangerous idealistic
propaganda.   It should have little trouble, however, in
explaining to the satisfaction of its own people, at least, that
it is fighting for a more elevated conception of public right
than its enemies.

So much for the war aims intended to appease the scruples
of a Liberal conscience.   Another class of war aims of a
general character, can reach a wider constituency.   The
collective egotism, or ethnocentrism, of a nation, makes it
possible to interpret the war as a struggle for the protection
and propagation of its own high type of civilization.   When a
nation is engaged in battle with a people whose technological
equipment is less destructive than its own, this form of
self-flattery is obviously founded upon clear differences.
The " whiteman's burden " has been carried lightly on the
shoulders of the British in India and Africa, and of the
Americans in Cuba and the Philippines.   But at first sight
it would appear paradoxical that a war between nations of
Western Europe should also assume the form of a war to
save civilization.   Their similarities are so much more
fundamental than their differences that a visitor from
another planet would undoubtedly bracket them together.

The explanation is to be found in the rise of literacy.
Literacy and elementary instruction have opened the cultural heritages of the nation to a larger portion of the community than ever before.   It was the " Yellow Press," which

popularized the idea in every country, but it was the wise men who used their acumen to prove it. On the 8th of August, 1914, the London *Evening Standard* shouted " Civilization at Issue," and the theme reverberated ever after. " Guerre contre les barbares," was simultaneously declared in France, while in Germany, the defence and nurture of *Kultur* became a duty and privilege of all good Germans. The consensus of German opinion is set out in a swollen flood of print, from which the following worthy specimens may be culled :

> Karl Lamprecht, *Krieg und Kultur* (Leipzig, 1914).
> Otto von Gierke, *Krieg und Kultur* (Berlin, 1914).
> Eugen Kühnemann, *Vom Weltreich des deutschen Geistes* (München, 1914).
> Oskar Fleischer, *Vom Kriege gegen die deutsche Kultur* (Frankfurt, 1915).
> Ernst Troeltsch, *Der Kulturkrieg* (Berlin, 1915).

In this list appear, among lesser luminaries, the foremost jurist and two of the most brilliant historians of the world. They were all convinced that the traditional Germany of philosophers and poets (*Denker und Dichter*) had of late added unto it, the practical gifts of political sagacity, exemplary fecundity, unremitting industry and monumental research, all of which compared more favourably with the atheism, sterility and giddiness of the decadent Latins, not to mention those sordid sportive, dawdling British. A brilliant example of this sort of thing is the volume called *Händler und Helden*, by Werner Sombart, the distinguished authority on modern, capitalism. The title of the book explains its animus : Traders and Heroes. The former are the British and the latter are the Germans, He advances the thesis that every war may be analysed into a war of beliefs. The present War is a struggle between the sordid British and the self-sacrificing, loyal, courageous and obedient Germans. The Englishman is incredibly narrow, utterly incapable of rising above the " realities " of the moment, as a glance at their philosophers from Bacon to Spencer will prove. To the trader life is but a series of bargains, and even science is commercialized. The whole empire is a great trading enterprise and the empire's wars are wars of pecuniary calculation. The Germans will never be conquered by this damning taint of commercialism, and their spirit will stamp it from the world. The war is a war of German Kultur, which must not be denied and cannot be denied by the trader.

The war can likewise be a war of race. Not only did the Germans of certain strata declare a war of Kultur, but they declared a war of race, and in this they were joined by certain elements elsewhere. The elements of the extreme right in France cherished the myth of a pure Gallic race, and *La Croix*, in its issue for August 15th, 1914, found that the heroic exertions of war are the

> ancient élan of the Gauls, the Romans and the French resurging within us. The Germans must be purged from the left bank of the Rhine. These infamous hordes must be thrust back within their own frontiers. The Gauls of France and Belgium must repulse the invader with a decisive blow, once and for all. The race war appears.

Urbain Gohier published *La race a parlé* at Paris in 1915. While war aims of this species are certain of a general vogue, they need re-enforcements of a more tangible and intimate kind. The nation as a whole, is divisible into an almost infinite number of constituent groups, which are in possession of special aspirations of their own. The war ought to be interpreted to them as something in which they have a stake, not only as members of the general group. The war ought to be fought to save business, family and church, and to add to prosperity, security and faith. Each interest should be encouraged to formulate war aims which point to the enemy of all who is, in fact, quite as much the enemy of each.

For the sake of the business men the war must appear as a profitable enterprise. L. G. Chiozza Money, M.P., published a statement in the London *Daily Chronicle* for August 10th, 1914, which is a pattern for this sort of thing. He wrote:

> Our chief competitor both in Europe and outside it will be unable to trade, and at the conclusion of the War the unmistakable antagonism which German aggression is everywhere arousing will help us to keep the trade and shipping we will win from her.

Sidney Whitman published a pamphlet, called *The War on German Trade. Hints for a Plan of Campaign* (London, 1914). Meanwhile, the economic groups of Germany swarmed with visions of tangible expansion in every direction. The Bund der Landwirte, der Deutsche Bauernbund, der Vorort der christlichen Bauernvereine, der Zentralverband deutscher Industrialer, der Bund deutscher Industrialer, and der Reichsdeutsche Mittelstandverband, joined in a monster petition on May 20th, 1915, to the Chancellor, in which they explained what they wanted.

The annexationist claims were : the whole of Belgium, Northern France to a line established from the mouth of the Somme straight eastward to the Belgian boundary, along the Maas, to its juncture with the Mosel in the Pagny-Toul region, thence through Lunéville east, along the Vosges to Belfort. The Departments of Pas de Calais and du Nord, half the Meuse Department, the greatest part of Meurthe and Moselle, part of Vosges and the Territory of Belfort, were thus contemplated additions to Germany. In the East a part of Livland, the largest and most densely inhabited part of Kurland, most of the Kovno district, the entire district of Suwalki, half of Lomza, all of Ploczk, a small slice of the Marschau district, half of Kalisch, a fourth of Pietrokoc, a small piece of Kielce—a total of 80,000 square kilometers, and five million people—were the annexationist claims. Adding this to the 50,000 square kilometers and the eleven million people demanded in the West, it appears that the German industrial and agrarian organizations were committed to the incorporation of 130,000 square kilometers and sixteen million non-Germans into the Imperial jurisdiction. The inhabitants of these areas were to be deprived of any political participation in the internal politics of Germany, and the large and middle-sized properties were to be transferred to German citizens at the cost of the defeated opponents of Germany.

Since the flaming vocabulary of religion still has the power to move the hearts of many men, it is a poor propagandist who neglects the spiritual and ecclesiastical interpretation of the War by the spokesmen of every sect. Each religious body must be brought to see in the discomfiture of the enemy, a triumph for its gods and priests and dogmas. Copious examples of the formulas which are appropriate to this end are to be found in the religious Press of every belligerent country. *La Croix*, the organ of the French clericals, identified the progress of France in the late War with the Kingdom of God. Writing in the feverish days of August, 1914, shortly after the alleged capture of Mulhouse by the French, it shouted,

> The story of France is the story of God.
> Long live Christ who loves the Franks ![1]

The Holy War, " La Guerre sainte," had been proclaimed the day before by *L'Echo de Paris*, when it reported how waves of spontaneous applause had broken out during solemn services at the Madelaine. *La Croix* published an interpretation of the War on August 15th. It is first of all a war of revenge, this revenge which we have desired for 43 years.

It is a colossal

duel between the Germans agains t the Latins and the Slavs.

It is a contest of

public morals and international law.

And, as a final climax,

Is it not a war of Catholic France against Protestant Germany ?

The Catholics of France were so zealous in the prosecution of the War that they aroused the suspicion of the radical

---

[1] " L'histoire de France est l'histoire de Dieu,
Vive le Christ qui aime les Francs ! " August 8.

elements in the country and quite a controversial literature sprang up. The pamphlet, *Les curés ont-ils voulu la guerre ?* (Did the priests want war ?), precipitated an acrimonious controversy.[1]

The German Catholics bitterly resented the attempt of the French clericals to monopolize the War. A literary relic of this dispute is the volume of able essays edited by Georg Pfeilschifter, *Deutsche Kultur, Katholizismus und Weltkrieg. Eine Abwehr des Buches " La Guerre allemande et le catholicisme."* (Freiburg, 1916.)

The churches of practically every description can be relied upon to bless a popular war, and to see in it an opportunity for the triumph of whatever godly design they choose to further. Some care must, of course, be exercised to facilitate the transition from the condemnation of wars in general, which is a traditional attitude on the part of the Christian sects, to the praise of a particular war. This may be expedited by securing suitable interpretations of the war very early in the conflict by conspicuous clericals ; the lesser lights will twinkle after. It was of some advantage to the war party in Britain to have such a statement as the following, from the Bishop of Hereford :

> Such a war is a heavy price to pay for our progress toward the realization of the Christianity of Christ, but duty calls, and the price must be paid for the good of those who are to follow us. That better and happier day when the people now under militarist rule shall regulate their own life is doubtless still so far away that an old man like myself can hardly hope to see it dawning, but amidst all the

[1] See Edouard Poulain, *Réfutation décisive* (1, *globale*, 2, *détaillée*) ; *onze rumeurs inflammées sur le clergé français* (Paris, 1916) ; Paul Feron-Vrau, *Les catholiques et la presse.*

burden of gloom and sorrow which this dreadful war lays upon us we can at least thank God that it brings that better day a long step nearer for the generation in front of us.[1]

The patriotic chorus of the gentlemen of the cloth in Germany reverberates again through the pages of the anthology prepared by Professor Bang during the War, and called *Hurrah and Hallelujah!* (New York, 1917.) Bang was a Danish professor of theology and took the pains to collect some of the German gems. Pastor Traub, P. de Lagards, and scores of other clericals unwittingly contributed to this book. All of it seems to be the grossest blasphemy to the enemies of Germany and the sincerest reverence to the friends of the German cause. Only the Liberal minority protests in Germany or elsewhere against the outpourings in its own behalf.[2]

The number of possible re-interpretations of a war is limited only by the number of special interests whose allegiance is offered or sought. To the economic and ecclesiastical groups already referred to could be added a constellation of artists, scientists, teachers, or sportsmen without end. The members of the talkative professions (preachers, writers, promoters) depend for a living upon their capacity to arouse an emotional response in the breasts of their *clientèle*. When the public is warmed up to fight, the clerical who treats the matter coldly is committing suicide, just as is the writer or the promoter. The circularity of response is established, for one interstimulates the other. The actor is the slave of his audience, though the audience is bound in temporary servitude to the actor.

Promoters can be relied upon to re-interpret the war aims

[1] London *Times*, August 12, 1914.
[2] See Hans Fülster, *Kirche und Krieg*, Heft 8 in *Kultur und Zeitfragen*.

of the groups with which they are identified. Thus certain musical promoters discovered that the War was really a war between German and British music. As Isidore de Lara wrote :

> The hour has come to put aside and to veil with crape the scores of the men who have crystallized in so unmistakeable a manner the spirit of the modern Huns. . .
>
> The future belongs to the young hero who will have the courage to exclude from his library all the works of Handel, Mendelssohn, Wagner, Brahms and Richard Strauss . . . who will draw from the depths of his own being tone pictures of all that is beautiful in the wonderful poetry of Great Britain, and find the vigorous rhythms that will tell of the dauntless spirit of those who go to death singing " Tipperary."[1]

Under the stress of war the nurses of the scrawny infant known as " Opera in English," were able to procure solid nourishment for their charge. To them, opera in German was a profanation, and the " Ring " was pronounced with the accent of Belgravia or not at all.

Certain American educators took advantage of the War to gather steam behind their pet projects of educational reform. The baneful influence of the German common school model upon American education was held up for universal execration, and the war for these educators became a sort of crusade to make the world safe from the *volksschule* and for the Junior High School.[2]

[1] " English music and German masters," *Fortnightly Review*, 103 : 847–853.

[2] Friedrich Schönemann in *Die Kunst der Massenbeeinflussung in den Vereinigten Staaten von Amerika*, Berlin and Leipzig, 1924, shows how every agency was mobilized to carry propaganda in the United States during and directly after the War. The school, the church, the women's club, the newspaper, the movie, the business club, the Ku Klux Klan, the American Defense Society, the National Security League, the American Legion, the " hereditary " patriotic societies (Sons of the American Revolution, etc.) all played their active part. Although the book is written in evident bitterness of spirit, it is an excellent piece of pioneering. This study avoids duplication as much as possible.

Over in Germany the tailors and dressmakers declared war upon the immoral fashions of decadent Paris and perfidious London. No longer was the matchless frame of the Fräulein to appear ridiculous in the simpering fluffs of Paris. She must be free and independent of the passing whims of Parisian mistresses.

In short, the active propagandist is certain to have willing help from everybody, with an axe to grind in transforming the War into a march toward whatever sort of a promised land happens to appeal to the group concerned. The more of these sub-groups he can fire for the War, the more powerful will be the united devotion of the people to the cause of the country, and to the humiliation of the enemy.

CHAPTER IV

SATANISM

WHEN the public believes that the enemy began the War and blocks a permanent, profitable and godly peace, the propagandist has achieved his purpose. But to make assurance doubly sure, it is safe to fortify the mind of the nation with examples of the insolence and depravity of the enemy. Any nation who began the War and blocks the peace is incorrigible, wicked and perverse. To insist directly upon these qualities is merely a precaution, and its chief effect is to make it more certain that the enemy could be capable of so monstrous a thing as an aggressive war. Thus, by a circularity of psychological reaction the guilty is the satanic and the satanic is the guilty.

The themes to be selected for emphasis depend upon the moral code of the nation whose animosity is to be aroused. But there are certain common denominators which can be counted upon to work in any situation. The opposing nation is nearly always demonstrably overbearing and contemptuous. The French Press was full of scornful thrusts at the presumptuous " Herrenvolk " just across the Rhine. These insolent and ridiculous people even took for their name a word " Allemagne," which, literally transcribed, is supposed to mean " all people ! " " Deutschland über alles " provoked exactly the same indignation in Downing Street and

Fleet Street that " Rule, Britannia ! " did in the Wilhelm-strasse and the Linden. Recruiting was stimulated in Great Britain at one time by playing up the alleged remark of the Kaiser, who referred to " the contemptible little English army."

The enemy is not only insolent. He is sordid. The Germans were perfectly sure that British envy was the root of the War, and, as for the United States, the economic motive was all too plain. As Charles A. Collman wrote in *Die Kriegstreiber in Wall Street* (Leipzig, 1917), the American manufacturers and bankers stayed out of the War, until their best customer, Great Britain, was threatened with insolvency, whereupon they proceeded to stampede the American public into the War, barely in time to save their accounts. The House of Morgan, with its overdraft to the British government of $400,000,000, was faced with certain ruin, having overstrained its credit to supply the British with munitions. Only the diversion of the first Liberty loan proceeds to Morgan saved him. The British Chancellor of the Exchequer, Bonar Law, made a clean breast of the British position in a speech which he delivered July 24th, 1917 :

> Indeed, it is an open secret that we had spent so freely of our resources that those available in America had become nearly exhausted when our great ally entered the struggle.

In December, 1916, the bare announcement that Germany was making overtures of peace sent stocks hurtling down. Bank credits were sharply curtailed and the Allied governments were able to renew their bills with the most extreme difficulty. The news of the diplomatic break with Germany on the 4th of February, 1917, sent Bethlehem Steel up 30 points. American industries, already geared for production to supply the Allies, had faced liquidation, readjustment and even ruin at the whispers of peace; they were able to breathe easily once more. Mr. Henry P. Davidson, a partner in J. P. Morgan and Company, had been one of the most active opponents of Germany's " insincere " peace offers; he had wished for American participation in the War in order to " cleanse us from our selfishness."[1]

The enemy is inherently perfidious. M. Felix Sartiaux wrote in the *Morale Kantienne et morale humaine* (1916) that

> One of the most subtle tendencies of the German character is the hypocritical lie, which appears under the guise of naïve sincerity, and justifies itself by the most incredible sophisms. . . . The judgment of a Latin historian, Villeius Peterculus has often been quoted. He found the ancient Germans a race of " born liars."[2]

The enemy conducts a lying propaganda. This theme is of particular importance. Unfavourable reports about allies, the heads of the army, the conditions at the front, and the bureaucracy are certain to leak past the censorship, or to spring full-blown inside the ramparts. Psychological barriers as well as physical barriers must be interposed between dangerous news and subversive responses. This psychological barrier consists in the suspicion that unfavour-

---

[1] These interpretations, which were current in Germany during the World War, can be read in English in J. K. Turner, *Shall It Be Again ?* and L. E. Rowley, *War Criminals* (Privately Published, Lansing, Michigan, 1924).
[2] Page 408.

able news is likely to be a cunning specimen of enemy propaganda. If this supposition can be planted firmly in the public mind, a mighty weapon has been forged against disunity and defeatism.

The Germans were aghast at the efficiency of Allied propaganda and they undertook to steel their people against it by protesting loudly against the official French and British Press and Press services. Rudolf Rotheit declared that one of the conditions of peace must be the emancipation of the World Press from the clutches of enemy telegraphic agencies. He wrote *Die Friedensbedingungen der deutschen Presse—Los von Reuter und Havas* (Berlin, 1915). Even the schools had such copying exercises as " Reuter's Agency, the fabricator of War lies." The British Press was the theme of Paul Dehn's study, entitled *England und die Presse* (Hamburg, 1915). The Germans took Northcliffe as the symbol of the British Press and poured vials of abuse on his head.

The cry of German propaganda in France was loud and insistent. Certain newspapers, even in the capital, were suspected of contaminating the French mind to suit German purposes. A more or less typical exposure of German methods is contained in *Le Matin* for October 24th, 1917. M. Louis Forest accuses the Germans of spending money to influence the Press abroad. He calls attention to the book of an Alsatian, which had exposed the German system before the War. Even during the Franco-Prussian War, the Germans had their friends in Parisian newspaper offices. After reviewing the evidence of past and present activity, he draws this conclusion :

everyone can determine for himself whether the present
German system is new or old. If to us it appears new, it
is because we are ignorant of such things.[1]

The enemy is quarrelsome, crude and destructive. MM.
Tudesq and J: Dyssord published *Les Allemands peints par
eux-mêmes* in November, 1917. Heine was the authority
for the remark that

> Christianity has softened to a certain degree this brutal
> belligerent ardour of the German, but has been unable to
> destroy it entirely.

Especially, exclaim the French editors, their proclivity
to destroy cathedrals, which has been amply confirmed by
the bombardment of Rheims, the burning of Belgian churches
and of cathedrals in Lorraine. Goethe had acknowledged
that

> We, the Germans, are of yesterday. For a century it
> is true that we have made substantial progress in civiliza-
> tion, but centuries will yet pass before our peasants will
> have the ideas or the spirit of a civilization sufficiently
> advanced to enable them to render homage to beauty as
> did the Greeks.

Schopenhauer blushes to belong to their race.

The enemy is atrociously cruel and degenerate in his
conduct of the War. A handy rule for arousing hate is, if
at first they do not enrage, use an atrocity. It has been
employed with unvarying success in every conflict known to
man. Originality, while often advantageous, is far from

---

[1] This may be read now with a certain amusement, for the Russian
documents have revealed the extent to which the Russian government
bought a large percentage of the French Press support which it enjoyed
in pre-war days. See the *Livre Noir* in particular, and the subsequent
articles in *L'Humanité*.

indispensable. In the early days of the War of 1914 a very pathetic story was told of a seven-year old youngster, who had pointed his wooden gun at a patrol of invading Uhlans, who had dispatched him on the spot. This story had done excellent duty in the Franco-Prussian War, over forty years before. But many of the most successful tales have a far more venerable history. There is one about the Turks, which had rattled down Christendom since the first crusades. According to this account, a tub full of eyes was discovered at a certain point, where captives were being tortured for the amusement of Turkish generals.

Stress can always be laid upon the wounding of women, children, old people, priests and nuns, and upon sexual enormities, mutilated prisoners and mutilated non-combatants. These stories yield a crop of indignation against the fiendish perpetrators of these dark deeds, and satisfy certain powerful, hidden impulses. A young woman, ravished by the enemy, yields secret satisfaction to a host of vicarious ravishers on the other side of the border. Hence, perhaps, the popularity and ubiquity of such stories.

While all atrocity stories show a family resemblance, and the old stand-bys can be relied upon, no classification should be regarded by the practical propagandist as more than suggestive. A certain fringe of novelty is always permissible, because the conditions of warfare are never precisely the same. Since the discovery of germs the enemy may be accused of infecting wells, cattle, and food, not to speak of wounds. A booklet on *Microbe-Culture at Bucharest* was put out in London in 1917, and covered the subject very nicely. If the enemy shows signs of believing that a cam-

paign of frightfulness is sound military strategy, there need
be no hesitation about calling God and man to witness that
such an abomination is the new-born creation of the dia-
bolical enemy. It was the absence of any opportunity for
effective contradiction in wartime which made it possible
for Professor Lavisse, for instance, to proclaim in the
Pratique et doctrine de la guerre allemande that

> Not one of our military writers taught the doctrine
> of the *guerre atroce.*

After peace came it was possible for another Frenchman,
Démartial, to procure a hearing in the interest of veracity
and to recall attention to a three-volume tome (*Vaincre*) by
the French officer Montaigne, in which this thesis was
defended :

> Terrify ; and in order to terrify, destroy. One sets out
> to kill, one shoots to kill, one leaps at the throat of the
> enemy but to kill, and one kills until there is nothing left
> to kill.[1]

Americans did not think it worth while to recall the
theory of war entertained by General Sheridan. He visited
Bismarck at the field headquarters of the Prussian Army
in France, in 1870, and declared,

> The proper strategy consists in the first place in inflicting
> as telling blows as possible upon the enemy's army, and
> then causing the inhabitants so much suffering that they
> must long for peace, and force their government to demand
> it. The people must be left nothing but their eyes to weep
> with over the war.[2]

[1] Cited on page 19 of G. Démartial, *Comment on mobilisa les consciences.*
" Umano," an Italian jurist, publishes an anonymous collection of statements by public men during the War which he regards as unfounded in
connection with his diffuse yet interesting study called *Positiva scienza di
governo,* 1922.
[2] Busch, *Bismarck,* I : 128.

It was likewise perfectly safe for President Poincaré to flay the barbarous Germans for dropping bombs upon defenceless women and children. Very few among the Allied peoples knew, and very few of them, had they known, would have cared, that on the 26th of June, 1916, French and English aviators dropped bombs upon Karlsruhe, killing or wounding 26 women and 124 children, or that on the 22nd of September, 1915, the Allied bombers had taken a toll of 103 victims in a raid upon the same city. In the fever of combat the news of the slaughter of enemy non-combatants is apt to be met by the exulting cry that the " whelps and dams of murderous foes " are no more, to quote a chivalrous line of Swinburne, when he heard about the frightful mortality in the concentration camps for Boer women and children in South Africa.

It was equally safe for the Allies to declare that it could only have occurred to a German Hun to organize a campaign of systematic destruction of machinery, warehouses, bridges and railroads in a region from which they were retreating. There was no one to call attention to the recommendations of the *Engineer*, a reputable British technical periodical, in its issue for September 25th, 1914, to the effect that the army ought to break up the equipment and to raze the factory of every German industry which the fortunes of war might bring into their hands. German competition after the War would thus be seriously crippled.[1] Nor was the destruction by the Allies of the oil properties during their retreat through Rumania conspicuously interpreted to the people as other than a smart stroke to cheat the enemy.

[1] Cited by Démartial as cited, p. 24.

A catalogue of the crimes which the enemy has been held to have perpetrated in the past ought to stimulate the ingenuity more than the imitativeness of the propaganda expert. The suggestions referred to here are by no means exhaustive. During the late War innumerable schemes for classifying enemy outrages were invented. As a random sample one may select the first large and important atrocity brochure put out by the French Government.[1]

German sins were sorted into bins which were labelled thus :

    1. Violation of the neutrality of Luxemburg and Belgium.

    2. Violation of French Frontier before the Declaration of War.

    3. Killing of prisoners and wounded.

    4. Looting, arson, rape, murder.

    5. Use of forbidden bullets.

    6. Use of burning liquids and asphyxiating gas.

    7. Bombarding of fortresses without notice and of unfortified towns ; the destruction of buildings consecrated to Religion, Art, Science and Charity.

    8. Treacherous Methods of Warfare.

    9. Cruelties inflicted on civil population.

Dr. Ernst Müller-Meiningen, a member of the German Reichstag, compiled the sins of the Entente in *Der Weltkrieg und der Zusammenbruch des Völkerrechts*, which had passed through a third revised edition by the middle of 1915. The general scheme of organization is indicated in the Table of Contents :

    1. The Neutrality of Belgium (How Belgium connived secretly with the Allies).

[1] République Française, *Documents rélatifs à la guerre 1914–15. Rapports et Procès-verbaux d'enquête de la commission instituée en vue de constater les actes commis par l'ennemi en violation du droit des gens.* Paris, 1915.

2. Mobilization and the Morality of Nations.

3. Violation of the Congo Acts.   The Colonial War.

4. The Employment of barbarous and warlike tribes in a European War.

5. The Violation of the Neutrality of the Suez Canal.

6. The Breach of Chinese Neutrality by Japan and England's Assault upon Kiao-Chau.

7. The use of Dum-Dum Bullets and the like.

8. Treatment of Diplomatic Representatives by the Triple Entente Countries in Violation of International Law. Acts of Diplomatic Representatives of the Triple Entente in Violation of International Law.

9. Non-observances and Violations of Red Cross Rules on the Part of the Triple Entente States.

10. Franc-Tireur Warfare and the Maltreatment of the Defenceless before and after the Declaration of War.   Also the Imprisonment of Civilians.

11. Unlawful and Inhumane Methods of Conducting War Practised by the Hostile Armies and the Governments of the Triple Entente and Belgium.

12. The Russian Atrocities in East Prussia in especial.

13. Jewish Pogroms and Other Russian Atrocities in Poland, Galicia, the Caucasus, etc.

14. The " Spirit " of the Troops of the Triple Entente. Plundering, and Destruction of their own country's Property. Self-Mutilations.   Verdicts upon the Troops of the Triple Entente by their own Officers.

15. The Destruction and Misuse of Telegraph Cables.

16. Further Details as to the Vendetta of Lies of the Press of the Triple Entente.   A Method of Waging War contrary to all International Law.   The French " Art of War."

17. The Bombardment of Towns and Villages from Aeroplanes.   The use of shells that develop Gas.

18. English Business Moral and the Code of English Creditors.   Deprivation of the Legal Rights of Germans in Russia and France.

19. Breaches of Neutrality on the Seas by England and the Other States of the Triple Entente.   Contraband of War.   Blockades, etc.

(Condensed.)

The quantitative methods of modern social science were applied to the atrocity problem as the War went on. In a report prepared for the Serbs about Austro-Hungarian atrocities the first plate, which summarizes the investigation is entitled, " Statistics of Atrocities." It is limited to the districts of Potzerie, Matchva, Yadar and certain others. Women and children are recorded in parallel columns, and the number of cases relating to each item is recorded. The items are :

> Executed or otherwise shot, Bayoneted or knifed, Throats cut, Killed, Burnt alive, Killed in massacre, Beaten to death with rifles or sticks, Stoned to death, Hanged, Disembowelled, Bound and tortured on the spot, Missing, Carried off as prisoners, Wounded, Arms cut off or broken, Legs cut off or broken, Noses cut off, Ears cut off, Eyes gouged out, Sexual parts mutilated, Skin torn in strips, Flesh or scalp removed, Corpses cut into small pieces, Breasts cut off, Women violated.

Certain special items, such as the use of explosive bullets, which were not susceptible of statistical treatment, were dealt with in qualitative terms.[1] To the impact of the quantitative method is added the dramatization of the individual case. The book is copiously embellished with horror-photographs of mutilated corpses and devastated villages.

There is a certain technical advantage in varying the form of the atrocity account. Sometimes a victim may be permitted to tell his own story, as in the case of a distinguished Belgian scholar who was condemned by the Ger-

[1] Kingdom of Serbia, *Report upon the atrocities committed by the Austro-Hungarian Army during the first invasion of Serbia*, by R. A. Reiss, London, 1916.

mans to forced labour and told his experiences in *Through the Iron Bars* (London, 1917). William Caine published an alleged interview with a victim of the German invasion, called *Monsieur Sagotin's Story* (London, 1917). The misadventure of a single person was related by W. T. Hill in *The Martyrdom of Nurse Cavell.*[1] The neutral witness always speaks with some authority, and Dr. De Christmas testified to the sad lot of the French prisoners in Germany as he visited them. His was called *Le Traitement des Prisonniers Francais en Allemagne* (Paris, 1917). Admissions by an enemy are always useful, and the French published the captured diary of a non-commissioned German officer, in which the cruelties perpetrated by officers on soldiers and civilians were written down. The diary was edited by Louis-Paul Alaux, and published in 1918, under the title *Souvenirs de guerre d'un sous-officer allemand.* The record of a *German Deserter's War Experience* was published in New York, 1917.

An excellent device which was used by the British to lend weight to their stories of German atrocities was to constitute a commission of men with international reputations for truthfulness to collect evidence and deliver findings. The British, with an eye not alone upon their own populace, but upon the American people, delivered a stroke of genius by appointing the so-called Bryce Commission. *The Evidence and Documents laid before the Committee on Alleged German Outrages* (London, 1915) was the *magnum opus* of the War on this front. The brochure on *German War Practices*, which was published by the Com-

---

[1] The German public believed that Miss Cavell was a spy, incidentally.

mittee on Public Information in the United States in 1916, was one of the last of the innumerable versions of this report.

Yet another form in which propaganda complaints may be made against the enemy is in the controversial statement or pamphlet. Dr. Max Kuttner remonstrated with a former pupil of his who had lent his pen to the French " calumnies " in a little booklet called *Deutsche Verbrechen?* . . . (in reply to) Joseph Bédier, *Les crimes allemands d'après temoignages allemands* (Bielefeld und Leipzig, 1915). Had not this Frenchman once been taught the importance of weighing evidence? Hubert Grimme took a similar line in his remarks on *Ein böswilliger Sprachstumper* (Münster, 1915). Nobody ever supposed that these pamphlets would produce repentance in France, but they serve to keep alive the spirit of virtuous indignation in Germany. To ask whether the Germans were criminals was like announcing a sermon on the subject, " Are Churchmen Hypocrites ? " The answer is a flattening and resounding negative which readily passes over into an indignant criticism of the perfidy of those who dare insinuate such a thing.

Before taking leave of the unsavoury subject of atrocities another principle must be brought out. It is always difficult for many simple minds inside a nation to attach personal traits to so dispersed an entity as a whole nation. ‖They need to have some individual on whom to pin their hate.‖ It is, therefore, important to single out a handful of enemy leaders and load them down with the whole decalogue of sins.

No personality drew more abuse of this sort in the last

War than the Kaiser. The London *Evening News* christened the Kaiser the " Mad Dog of Europe " on the 6th of August, and the " War Lord " a little while thereafter. Austen Harrison wrote about *The Kaiser's War* (London, 1914). The *Liberté* of Paris took pains in the issue of November 24th, 1916, to identify William II. with the Beast of the Apocalypse, as foreseen by St. John. It appeared that upon the basis of researches, conducted by an English savant, the number of the Beast was 666, and the Kaiser's number was just this. The word Kaiser has six letters. Place them one beneath the other in a column. At the left of each number, record the place in the alphabet, which is occupied by each of these letters. Thus " K," the eleventh letter in the alphabet, is placed beside six, to make 116. The completed columns sum up to 666, the mystic number.[1]

It would be possible to multiply the individual adjectives which can serve as the themes for injurious propaganda against a nation, but it is now more to the point to suggest some of the methods by which the whole of the indictment can be presented synthetically. There are some, who do not hesitate to indict a whole civilization at a single gesture, and these mentalities may be relied upon to furnish systematic treatises upon such subjects as *Civilisés contre Allemands*. This particular book was published in Paris in 1915, by the Frenchman, Jean Finot, who had published an excellently objective treatise on race prejudice before the War. In the same strain wrote the eminent historian, Ernest Lavisse, in his *Kultur et Civilisation* (1915), and

---

[1] Repeated in Graux, *Les fausses nouvelles de la grande guerre,* I : 282. Former Ambassador J. W. Gerard criticized the Kaiser in *My Four Years in Germany,* New York, 1917, and *Face to Face with Kaiserism,* New York, 1918. The dentist Arthur N. Davis wrote about *The Kaiser as I Knew Him,* New York and London, 1918.

André Saures in *Nous et Eux* (1915). Mr. Rudyard Kipling said in the columns of *The Morning Post* (London) of June 22nd, 1915:

> But, however the world pretends to divide itself, there are only two divisions in the world to-day—human beings and Germans.

In what purported to be a scientific treatise on the Instincts of the Herd in Peace and War (London, 1917), Trotter solemnly said,

> The incomprehensibility to the English of the whole trend of German feeling and expression suggests that there is some deeply-rooted instinctive conflict of attitude between them.   One may risk the speculation that this conflict is between socialized gregariousness and aggressive gregariousness.[1]

Mr. John Cooper Powys replied to Professor Münsterberg under the title, *The Menace of German Culture* (London, 1915).   The Germans were heaping up a vast literature of self-exaltation about the theme, Kultur.   An inspection of this list of selected titles from German output will reveal something of its scope and purport :

Herm. Cohen, *Ueber das Eigentümliche des deutschen Geistes* (Berlin, 1915).

E. Bergmann, *Die weltgeschichtliche Mission der deutschen Bildung* (Gotha, 1915).

Rudolf Eucken, *Die weltgeschichtliche Bedeutung des deutschen Geistes* (Stuttgart, 1914).

R. v. Delius, *Deutschlands geistige Weltmachtstellung* (Stuttgart, 1915).

J. A. Lux, *Deutschland als Welterzieher* (Stuttgart, 1914).

Herausgeg. v. Karl Hönn, *Der Kampf des deutschen Geistes im Weltkrieg. Dokumente des deutschen Geisteslebens aus der Kriegszeit* (Gotha, 1915).

[1] Page 174.

German assurance and self-esteem was buttressed by the testimony of a cloud of foreign witnesses. Björn Björnson, Scandinavian writer, paid a tribute called *Vom deutschen Wesen. Impressionen eines Stammesverwandten*, 1914–17 (Berlin, 1917). Houston Stewart Chamberlain, ex-patriated Englishman, rallied to the defence of the *Deutsches Wesen* (München, 1916). In his earlier writings he had exclaimed, " If there is in the world a peaceful, well-behaved, pious people, it is the Germans. In the last forty-three years, not a single man in the whole country has desired war—no, not one." England had been led into the War by the unscrupulous machinations of a King who was a tool of a cunning diplomat. England was no longer the land of liberty, but the slave of a vicious oligarchy.[1] Ferdinand Tönnies, a celebrated German sociologist, brought together all the imperialistic utterances of British statesmen in his book about England.[2] The business of editing anthologies of incriminating remarks thrived all during the War. Jean Ruplinger published a collection of German War utterances, under the title, *Also sprach Germania*. The book appeared in Paris in 1918, with a preface by Edouard Herriot. William Archer compiled the *Gems of German Thought*, which was published in 1917.

A great mass of specialized studies upon different features of the life and character of another country is welcome in war. The aged philosopher and psychologist Wilhelm Wundt compared the philosophical ideals of every nation,

---

[1] His earlier essays were published in England in 1915 under the title of *The Ravings of a Renegade*.

[2] An English edition was brought out in New York in 1915 under the title, *Warlike England As Seen by Herself*.

greatly to the advantage of Germany, in a brochure entitled, *Die Nationen und ihre Philosophie* (Leipzig, 1914). In particular, Baron Cay von Brockdorff took care to expose the truth about Bergson, as he saw it, in *Die Wahrheit über Bergson* (Berlin, 1917). In the United States, John Dewey unintentionally did great service to those who were drumming up sentiment against Germany by ringing the changes on certain aspects of German philosophy in his book on *German Philosophy and Politics* (New York, 1915), which had a new vogue when America went to War. If the history of Prussia was interpreted as a record of ruffian robberies by Allied scholars, the story of British imperialism was a stench in the nostrils of the Germans. Some incriminating morsels were assembled in books about Persia and India, such as the *Englische Dokumente zur Erdrosselung Persiens* (Berlin, 1917), and *Indien unter der britischen Faust* (Berlin, 1916). The real meaning of political freedom was·clarified by A. O. Meyer, who discovered that real freedom was in Germany and not in England, and wrote *Deutsche Freiheit und englischer Parlamentarismus* (München, 1915). The Belgian Fr. De Hovée intended to compliment the British educational system, when he compared it to the disadvantage of the German system, by writing that its aim might be summarized in the slogan

Be good, my pretty maid, and let who will be clever.

His book was *German and English Education* (London, 1917). While Germany was yet at peace with America, Dr. Karl Henning published a scurrilous pamphlet on America, called *Die Wahrheit über America* (Leipzig, 1915) which was subsequently useful when War came. Henning devoted most of his attention to the family and the educational system in the United States. He combed the reports of some of the municipal vice commissions for juicy stories about sex offences committed by children and reproduced these as typical of the standards of American life. One prize exhibit was a letter, which he said was in his possession, and was written by an eight-year old girl to a boy of the same age. It was :

> Dear Arthur,—I will come over to-night, shall I ? Do you love me ? I love you very dearly and to-night we will go to a show and stay till midnight and we will dance at a theatre for a long time and then we will come home and you can sleep with me till morning and next Sunday we will go horse-riding. Your sweetheart, M. (Page 54.)

Now monographs of every variety reach a certain restricted audience, and if the wider circles of the public are to be touched by synthetic representations of the life of another country, the form must be personal and dramatic and literary. Of this sort of thing a book put out in England during the War may well serve as a model. It was plausible, well-written, and utterly devastating. I have been told by more than one member of the German propaganda service, that they considered it the best piece of propaganda work gotten out by the Allies in the course of the War. This was *Christine*, by Alice Cholmondeley (New York, 1917). It purported to be an authentic collection of letters written by a music student in Germany to her mother in England. The girl was a talented violinist and in May, 1914, went over to study with a great German master. She was bubbling with enthusiastic anticipation of art and life in Germany.

She wrote her Berlin letters from an address in Lützowstrasse, where a Pension was known to be.

All is buoyance and happiness until, by degrees, German civilization begins to make itself known to her. The police are boorish and haughty. Her music master is secretly scornful of the whole German régime. The talk at the Pension is about clean Berlin, and slummy London. She is held more or less personally responsible for the Boer War. She is pestered by all sorts of irritating rules and regulations, for she is not allowed to practise on the Sabbath. Rules are typical of Germany, and she finds a girl acquaintance celebrating the birthday of her father, whom she despised, five years after his death. Her lamp is taken away at 10 p.m. and she is left with a candle. Snobbishness abounds. A Countess patronizes the arts, but will not permit her daughter to become contaminated. A young German of high birth longs to become a musician, but the caste conventions make an officer of him. The children kill themselves in Germany because of overwork in the schools. She is elbowed by men and boys when she walks abroad alone. The pros and cons of Weltpolitik follow her everywhere. An ominous sense of impending war pervades everything. The lower classes grovel in servile respect before the upper classes. The drill, perhaps, does it. Unmarried girls are not supposed to ask questions in conversations, but to keep discreetly silent and unobtrusive. A rural pastor lectures her on the English love of money bags. She meets a staff officer, who ominously advises her to ask the Council of her Sussex village to straighten the road for heavy traffic. An expectant mother prays for a boy baby, so that she can be the mother of a soldier.   She finds the German aristocrats so middle class.   She becomes engaged to the charming young officer with musical frustrations.   As the international crisis approaches, she sees wild orgies of joy at the imminence of War.   Her violin master has his mouth stuffed by receiving a Royal decoration.   Her marriage is blocked by the superior officer of her betrothed.   She flees to escape internment and is stopped on the border.   A young subordinate forces her to wait in the sun for two hours, and she gets double pneumonia, dying at Stuttgart on the 8th of August, 1914.   All the facts about German life are floated in a wave of gush about music and mother.   The whole thing is marvellously executed, and the book had a tremendous circulation among women and school children in Allied and neutral countries.   It is typical of the circumstantial-sentimental type of thing which can be placed in the fiction columns of a woman's magazine or in the book stalls.   By such a thing does the opposing nation become His Satanic Majesty, the Enemy.

The cult of satanism thus arises and feeds on hate.   Vengeance is Mine, saith the Lord, and the Lord is working through us to destroy the Devil.   The stirring stanzas of Lissauer's famous " Hymn of Hate " expose all this in its pristine nudity.

> Hate by water and hate by land ;
> Hate of the heart and hate of the hand ;
> We love as one, we hate as one ;
> We have but one foe alone,—England.

All the specific means of conquering the Evil One are, and should be, glorified.   The cult of battle requires that every form of common exertion (enlistment, food-saving, munition making, killing the enemy) should have the blessing of all the holy sentiments. In Christian countries precautions must be taken to calm the doubts of those who undertake to give such a book as the Bible an inconvenient interpretation. It is always expedient to circulate the arguments of the preachers and priests who are willing to explain how you can follow Jesus and kill your enemies. There are always enough theological leaders to undertake the task, since it is only the small sects, usually regarded as fanatical, who see any serious difficulty in the problem. In the German war literature are to be found many books which were written to remove doubts from those hesitant souls, who hated to shoot worse than they hated the English. Theodore Birt reassured the Christians who were perplexed by the exhortation to " Love your enemies " in *Was heisst " Liebet eure Feinde " ? Ein Wort zur Beruhigung* (Marburg, 1915). W. Walther wrote a popular treatise for the benefit of the Lutherans. It is called *Deutschlands Schwert durch Luther geweiht* (2 Aufl., Leipzig, 1915). Otto Albrecht found a forecast of victory in Luther, *Eine Kriegspredigt aus Luthers Schriften* (1914).

It is also useful to justify war in general on ethical rather than exclusively religious grounds. The eminent Rudolf Eucken praised the moral power of war in *Die sittlichen Kräfte des Krieges* (Leipzig, 1914), and Theodor Elsenhaus lauded it as a great teacher in *Der Krieg als Erzieher* (Dresden, 1914). Theodor Kipp saw no antithesis between the idea of might and right, the important thing being to make the right mighty, as he contended in *Von der Macht des Rechts* (Berlin, 1914).

The justification of war can proceed more smoothly if the hideous aspects of the war business are screened from public gaze. People may be permitted to deplore war in the abstract, but they must not be encouraged to paint its horrors too vividly. In fact, there is place for such items as this one, which appeared in the American Press during the early days of the Spanish-American War :

> DEATH RATE HAS GROWN LESS. Fearful Record of Trafalgar's Days has never been equalled. Machine Gun's Moral Effect. Modern guns less destructive than flint locks, dart, or javelin.[1]

Better yet, of course, is the interpretation of the war in terms of heroism, good fellowship, smartness and picturesqueness. In the late War, an artist like Muirhead Bone could be relied upon to present *The Western Front* in softened sketches. The humorous magazines and books help to banter away the realities of battle and they profit from the impulse to turn one's head away from a spectacle which, if completely realized, might well prove unbearable. A Bruce Bairnsfather is worth at least an Army Corps.[2] Popular accounts of how the military machinery works give the public a sense of knowing just how things get on ; of course, the writers should be careful to keep too much blood from getting mixed in the story. Such writers as Bernard Shaw, H. G. Wells, and Arthur Conan Doyle, were sent to visit the British officials and they came back with

---

[1] Louisville *Courier-Journal*, June 26, 1898.
[2] See, for instance, *Bullets and Billets*, N.Y., 1917.

discreet accounts of how they felt about it. Ludwig Gang-hofer described all the German fronts in a series of books.

It is the letters and books written by actual fighters to which the most importance is attached. Harold R. Peat (*Private Peat*) and Sergeant Guy Empey (*Over the Top*) explained the actual conduct of modern war to Americans. Donald Hankey (*A Student in Arms*) was a soldier who saw the War through the lenses of a moral and religious idealist, and his book struck many responsive chords in America and England. This same quality pervaded the work of certain other writers, such as *Carry On?* by Coningsby Dawson. A whimsical, determined note in Ian Hay's *First Hundred Thousand* sent it through the English-speaking world, as soon as it fell from the Press.

Tales of individual adventure kept the old spell of romance about war. One soldier told *Was ich in mehr als* 80 *Schlachten und Gefechten erlebte* (Berlin, 1916). Pat O'Brien told how he escaped from the Germans in *Outwitting the Hun* (New York, 1916). Dr. Th. Preyer tells how he managed to return home from New York in *Von New York nach Jerusalem und in die Wüste* (Berlin, 1916). Paul König related the exploits of the submarine which crossed the Atlantic in *Die Fahrt der Deutschland* (Berlin, 1917). Marcel Hadaud caught the atmosphere of air battle in *En plein vol* (Paris, 1916). The *Zeppeline über England* met with a warm reception in Germany in 1916, as did *Kapitän-leutnant Freiherr von Förstner als U-Bootes Kommandant gegen England*. Von Mücke's story of the *Emden* was one of the most popular books of the War. Kurt Agram told the sensational story of the 100,000 Germans, who were banished to Siberia by the Russian Government, and of how he managed to escape, in *Nach Sibirien mit* 100,000 *Deutschen*. How he managed to reach the Fatherland from the besieged colonies was the theme of Emil Zimmermann, *Meine Kriegsfahrt von Kamerun zur Heimat.*

Special collections of letters from the front were prepared in all countries. *Der deutsche Krieg in Feldpostbriefen, Soldier's Tales of the Great War*, and similar collections ran into several volumes. Special volumes were continually appearing, such as Charles Foley, *La vie de la guerre* (Paris, 1917), in which the War letters first published in *L'Écho de Paris* are brought within one cover. Sketches of the front were always welcome when done with any literary skill, and Henry de Forge, *Ah! la belle France !* (Paris, 1916), Maurice Grandolphe, *La marche à la victoire* (Paris, 1915), or Max Buteau, *Tenir. Récits de la vie de Tranchées* (Paris, 1918) were ample to satisfy the demand.[1]

Professional people of various kinds are able to reach their own public, and should be encouraged to write. Aug. A. Lemaître, pastor at Liévin, and of Swiss origin, gave his story of *Un an près des champs de bataille de l'Artois* (Edité par la société centrale évangélique, Paris). J. Emile Blanche's *Cahiers d'un artiste* (Paris, 1917) touched the artistic fraternity. Teachers, doctors and nurses, not to speak of engineers and chemists, belong to the ranks of those, who can usually describe what they see, with some reserves about the unpleasant.

During the first few weeks of the War those elements in

---

[1] Boyd Cable performed the difficult task of squeezing stories out of official communiqués. In his *Between the Lines* and other books, a dull, dry extract from an official despatch was polished up into a story.

the business community who required some coddling before they would face realities, were fed on such catchwords as " Business as Usual." This phrase sprang up quickly in England, where it had a short vogue before succumbing to facts and ridicule. Mr. Tom Bruce Jones brought out a pamphlet on *The Danger of Britain's Invasion, and how it may be met whilst carrying on " business as usual "* (Falkirk, 1914). On the 11th of August, the phrase appeared in the London *Daily Chronicle* in the letter from H. E. Morgan of W. H. Smith and Sons. Thus are all barriers down to the glorification of all the means necessary to the overcoming of evil by force.

CHAPTER V

THE ILLUSION OF VICTORY

THE fighting spirit of a nation feeds upon the conviction that it has a fighting chance to win. The enemy may be dangerous, obstructive, and satanic, but if he is sure to win, the moral of many elements in the nation will begin to waver and crumble. The animosity of a discouraged nation may be diverted to a new object, and the nation may be so busy hating the ruling class of its own country or its own allies, that it simply ceases to hate the technical enemy, and military collapse ensues.

The illusion of victory must be nourished because of the close connection between the strong and the good. Primitive habits of thought persist in modern life, and battles become a trial to ascertain the true and the good. If we win, God is on our side. If we lose, God may have been on the other side. To bow to necessity is to bow to the right, unless the universe is itself evil, or unless this can be interpreted as a temporary tribulation meted out to punish us for past sins or to cleanse us for future glory. In any case, defeat wants a deal of explaining, while victory speaks for itself.

The state of public expectation about the issue of the War depends upon the answer to the query, what is the relative strength of our side, and the enemy's side? From the propagandist point of view there are several striking examples of the way this question ought not to be answered. To insist upon the feebleness of the enemy, and to foster public expectation of his imminent collapse is to encourage hopes which may be indefinitely deferred, with the resulting danger of disenchantment, depression and defeat. During the first month of the late War Paris was left without exact news of the position of the struggling armies, and the most feverish rumours filled the void. Paris expected immediate victory. Had not von der Goltz admitted that the enervating life of the cities had already fostered the decadence of Germany? Had not General Keim declared that Germany could never have won in 1870 but for the circumstance that she outnumbered the French by one-third, a disparity which the presence of the English and the Belgians had now overcome? Were not Italy, Holland and Portugal on the verge of casting in their lot with the Entente? Were not enemy prisoners begging bread for themselves and oats for their horses? Were not strikes and riots breaking out in Berlin? Were not the soldiers driven to battle by their Prussian officers at the point of the pistol? Were not they deserting in droves, and had not a single French soldier on patrol frightened fifty Germans into surrender? Were not our horses drinking at the brooks in Lorraine?

After the report that Mülhausen had been captured on the 9th of August no more specific information was published until much later about the theatre of the War. Of what then did the newspapers write? Dr. Graux, a physician, kept a diary of War rumours, which has been published in five volumes. He answers the question thus:

Of German atrocities ?   That, alas, was true.   But also of
the correspondence of soldiers, a religious ceremony at the
Kremlin, the findings of a military commission of inquiry
at Belfort, our manner of treating prisoners, the Crown
Prince's wound—a false report—war correspondents, the
prohibition of Russian exports, Swiss neutrality, German
bluff, a patriotic address by M. Clémentel, the ambulance
of Madame Messimy, of Swiss volunteers, *les promenades
de Paris*, the conquest of Togo, Red Cross supplies, Americans maltreated in Germany !¹

But where were the Germans ?

It was not until the 20th that the *Matin* began to break
the news.   Its headline read :

ARE THEY AT BRUSSELS ?

As the truth began, in part, to filter through, wild rumours
clouded the sky.   Alarmists saw Germans in the Bois de
Boulogne.   On the 27th there appeared no official communiqué, and on the 28th the newspapers tried to plug the
gap by prophesying that

THE   TSAR   SOON   DICTATES   CONDITIONS   TO
GERMANY.

On the 29th the front seemed to be on the Somme, and
on the 30th the facts came out.   Hopes were meanwhile
nourished on the report that " Turpinite," a new and
deadly explosive, would annihilate the invader.

In Berlin the first twenty-five days of the War were
passed in a joyous delirium.   The papers were congested
with news of captured soldiers, captured guns, captured
flags.   More material of war was taken than in the whole

¹ The record of the first few days is found in Graux, *Les Fausses Nouvelles
de la Grande Guerre*, vol. 1.

campaign of 1870. The fall of Paris was but a matter of days.

The exaggerated optimism of those days reverberated in an undertone of accusation all during the War. Had not the public been grossly misled by its leaders? The proper way to manage the public, of course, is to insist upon the *ultimate* success of our cause. Both the French and the German commands were saved from complete loss of confidence by the thesis of " surprise attack " by the enemy, and this is an excellent theme for the propagandist to foster. If you win, you can afford to let the " surprise attack " slip out of mind, but if you are embarrassed, it is a very present help in time of trouble. The civilian population is ready to accept this thesis, because it knows perfectly well that it was plotting no war and, therefore, that the enemy must have been.

Among the Allied powers the official thesis was that Germany, armed to the teeth and crouched to spring, had suddenly, to the consternation of the peaceful and unprepared world, invaded Belgium and swept through Northern France before the pacific and astonished Allies could recover from the shock sufficiently to stem the attack.

So far as the truth is concerned, the fact seems to be that the talk about " surprise attack " and " unpreparedness " was grossly exaggerated for the purpose of covering up the failure of French strategy and of preventing the total eclipse of civilian moral. Such, at least, is the thesis of Jean de Pierrefeu, who, as the maker of official communiqués at General Headquarters during the War, was in a favourable position to ascertain the truth. After having connived at deception for the years of the War, he had undertaken to reveal the truth as he saw it in a book called *Plutarch Lied* (*Plutarque a-t-il menti ?*).   He says that the French General Staff had known for years that the German attack would be by way of Belgium, and that they had planned their strategy with this in mind, but that they were beaten in open combat, because their plan miscarried.   The High Command kept indispensable reinforcements from the Left, which was crumpling before the Germans, on the supposition that a French attack through Alsace would enable them to imperil the communications of the German armies in the West.   The French were hurled back in Alsace, swept aside in the West, their whole plan of campaign smashed into bits, and their very existence saved only by a boneheaded play on the part of the Germans.[1]

The thesis of surprise attack is rendered plausible to the civilian population by rumours of enemy spies.   Spy hunts are due to great excitement in the presence of a huge, new danger, which is magnified by the sense of personal frustration produced by the sense of inability to do anything effective toward dispelling the menace.   The peasants of Germany were excited by the wild tales of yellow automobiles which were supposed to be dashing from France across Germany, laden with gold for Russia.   They stretched iron chains across the roads and made it unhappy for many a poor tourist.   Military despatch riders in Great Britain were frequently stopped and lodged in gaol during the

---

[1] For the pre-war literature which forecasted and analysed the strategy of the War, see John Bakeless, *The Origin of the Next War*, ch. X.   For another side of a controversial issue, see Philp Neames, *German Strategy and the Great War*.

feverish days of the War.   The spy mania is a great inconvenience to many people, but it helps to arouse the community to a deeper sense of the necessity for joint action in the crisis.   Such books as that of William Le Queux, *Britain's Deadly Peril* (London, 1915) project the spy fear further into the conflict.

The theory of surprise attack must be associated with the thesis of our brilliant resistance to temporarily overwhelming odds, if undue pessimism is to be averted.   Our ultimate success is assured.   Our reserves of men and material and foreign friendship are greater than those of the enemy.   On these points, foreign testimony is particularly reassuring.   The French encouraged themselves by publishing the *Voix italiennes sur la guerre de* 1914–15 and the *Voix de l'Amérique latine* (Preface by Gomez Carillo) in 1916.   The English collected *Sixty American Opinions on the War* (1915), and welcomed Roosevelt's *Why America should join the Allies* (1915).   Ramsey Muir wrote an introduction to the English edition of *The War and the Settlement*, by Rignano, the eminent Italian philosopher (1916).   The Germans favoured the War correspondents of foreign countries before the Allies woke up to its importance, and they were usually sure of a rich harvest of clippings for reproduction in the home Press.   Sven Hedin, a Swede, wrote *With the German Armies in the West*, which was widely translated.   The Germans were assured of the active aid and sympathy of the Germans in the United States, according to the book by Karl Junger, called *Deutsch-Amerika mobil . . . !* (Berlin, 1915).   A Swiss neutral, Dr. J. Strebel, told the Germans about some encouraging signs of future collapse, which he

had observed in Allied countries. His *Reisebilder* was put
out at Lucerne and Berlin in 1915. A Swiss neutral, Paul
Balmer, told the French about some encouraging signs of
future collapse which he had observed in Germany. His
Les Allemands chez eux was put out at Paris in 1915. An
American pacifist had seen suffering in Germany at first
hand, and wrote *Short Rations* (by Madeleine Z. Doty)
which was published in New York in 1917.

Such cumulated fact and opinion may be supplemented
by prophecy. The famous *Almanach de Madame de Thèbes*
nourished the moral of certain classes of the French public
in the critical days of 1914. The *Figaro* published a prophecy on the 19th of August, 1914, which was supposed to
date from the year 1600. A certain Friar John foresaw that
an Anti-Christ by the name of William the Second would
succumb in the same territory where he forged his weapons.
Essen and Westphalia were undoubtedly meant.

Occasionally, a prophecy will inadvertently work both
ways. The Germans launched a prediction that victory
would rest with three emperors and three kings, which
clearly referred to Germany, Austria, Turkey, Bavaria,
Saxony and Bulgaria. The Entente was able to match
this array with Russia, India, Japan, Belgium, Italy and
Serbia.[1]

Prophecies for the more sophisticated members of the
community take on subtler forms. Thus Professor Lanessan
took a hand in explaining *Pourquoi les Germains seront
vaincus*, (Paris, 1915). In 1916 Lloyd George was said to
have remarked to Emile Vandervelde of Belgium that—

[1] 1 Graux, as cited, I : 244.

England declared war in 1914, began it in 1915, developed it in 1916 and will finish it in 1917.

It seems that in the main, however, the canny Welshman confined himself to the excellent formula:

We will finish the War when we have attained our objective.

There is a great advantage in having certain unofficial interpreters of the War to the public who can be relied upon to present matters in their most flattering light. Frank Symonds in the United States, Colonel Repington in England and Commander Rousset in France secured the confidence of the public and were of the greatest assistance to the authorities, for they were cogs in the machinery by which those interpretations least damaging to public moral were circulated. They were able to explain why retreats were " strategic retirements," and how evacuations could be " rectifications of the line."

One of the questions which rises in the conduct of the War is how to handle the news of losses. The possible policies vary all the way from complete suppression to immediate disclosure. When Winston Churchill was at the Admiralty he was characterized by the Chief Naval Censor as

a bit of a gambler, *i.e.*, he would hold on to a bit of bad news for a time on the chance of getting a bit of good news to publish as an offset, and I must say that it not infrequently came off ! On the other hand, there were days when it did not, and then there was a sort or " Black Monday " atmosphere about—a bad " settling day " sort of look on all our faces.

After he left I always pleaded for the immediate publication of disasters or, at any rate, that they should be made known as soon as the number of casualties had been reported and the relatives informed ; and this soon became more or less the practice.[1]

The British followed the policy of complete silence when they lost the battleship *Audacious* on the 27th of October, 1914, by a mine off the Irish coast.   It was never officially acknowledged while the War lasted, and was solemnly reported after the armistice.   The Germans were able to make a great deal of capital out of the reticence of the British in the early days, and it was not until the Jutland affair that the British were able, by a daring stroke, to recapture confidence at home and abroad.   The Germans announced by wireless on the 31st of May that they had won a great naval victory.   Damaged ships and messages to relatives began to come along the east coast of England, and silence was no longer feasible.   The official communiqué for the 2nd of June made a clean breast of the British losses as so far reported.   The shock was stupendous.   When the enemy losses began to come in later in the day, the general consternation was somewhat assuaged.   The Germans were slowly constrained to admit the truth.[2]

It is probably sound, on the whole, to reveal losses when they come, and to trust to the ingenious multiplication of favourable news to neutralize the effect.   Special problems arise in connection with losses which are known only in a general way to the enemy.   Brownrigg opposed the publica-

[1] Rear-Admiral Sir Douglas Brownrigg, *Indiscretions of the Naval Censor*, p. 13.
[2] Brownrigg tells the story from the British point of view in Chapter 4 of the book cited.

tion of British losses of merchant ships from enemy submarines and mines on the ground that the enemy would, in this way, be supplied with precise information that he would not otherwise get. The public demand for enlightenment on the progress of the submarine war was so insistent that a compromise was ultimately arrived at. At first, the number of ships lost per week was announced, with no further particulars, and later, the tonnage lost per week was substituted for the number of ships. This suggests a sound principle in dealing with such matters. When the losses are of such a character that the enemy cannot be entirely certain of them, the disclosure ought to take a summary and not a particularized form. A definite total is necessary in order to allay the wild exaggerations of alarmist whispers.

Another problem which arises in the conduct of war is how to treat new devices of warfare which it is proposed to introduce. Every new innovation by a belligerent is likely to be welcomed at home as a promise of victory, and to be condemned abroad as a crime against humanity. But there are exceptions to this rule, and for the sake of squeamish souls at home, who may deplore the introduction of particularly devastating measures, a careful campaign of preparation should be launched. If it is reported that the enemy has just adopted a new device, cries will arise instantly for its adoption as a measure of justifiable reprisal. Aerial bombardment and the use of gas were supposed by both the Allied and the German publics to be the product of the nefarious genius of the other side. The submarine was defended in Germany as a reply to the brutal British blockade which had so far disregarded the bounds of international law as to become a weapon of attack against the old and the very young, the women and the children, rather than against the fighting men. The Government defended the order to sink without warning, by telling how the Allies took advantage of the kind heart of a certain submarine commander. An English sailor, dressed in women's clothes, and with a bundle which appeared to be a baby, stood on the deck of a boat which a submarine had just stopped. The submarine came up to take off the unfortunate woman before sinking the ship, when the disguised sailor suddenly dropped a bomb on the submarine, destroying it instantly.

For those very numerous members of the nation who visualize war as a battle of goliaths, the propaganda of confidence in leaders is indispensable. It is a reassuring experience to read a well-written biography of a public character. Otto Krack wrote a popular *Life of Ludendorff*, and Harold Begbie glorified Kitchener in his book, *Kitchener, Organiser of Victory*. *General Paul von Hindenburg* was written up by Bernard von Hindenburg.

Reports of heroic achievement in routine or exceptional jobs strengthen the assurance of ultimate victory. To the tales from the trenches must be added the less dramatic tale of how the country is solidly behind the front in food saving, munition making, and relief work. Rudolf Hans Bartsch took a trip around Germany and described *Das deutsche Volk in schwerer Zeit*, a volume which was reassuring to the men at the front and encouraging to the civilians.

The will to win is intimately related to a chance to win. The thesis of ultimate victory is indispensable to the conduct of war, if discouragement is not to sap determination and to precipitate internal friction and strife.

CHAPTER VI

PRESERVING FRIENDSHIP

ONE prerequisite of a solid front against the enemy is cordial relations among allies. It is particularly important that allies should stimulate one another by emphasizing their strenuous exertion in the prosecution of the war. During the last War the effective entry of America into the struggle came before Italy had recovered from the collapse of Caporetto. Weary and discouraged, the Italian people were cynical of America's whole-hearted sincerity in making war. The Americans, so it was whispered about, are an industrial people, who have forgotten how to fight. They are unwilling to forsake their prosperous jobs for a post of danger. America had no army, did not want one, and could not raise one if she tried. Supposing that an army were actually raised, the submarines would sink all transports capable of bringing it to Europe. And, anyhow, American officers and soldiers were too inexperienced to matter much.[1]

The ringing keynote of American propaganda in Italy was, therefore, the invincible determination of America to smash the Central Powers, as revealed by her war preparations. The New York Office of the Committee on Public Information prepared items of news which were distributed through the Agenzi Stefani, the largest Press

[1] On the Italian situation, see C. E. Merriam, " American Publicity in Italy," *American Political Science Review*, November, 1919.

Association. These items had to do with military preparation, ship building, food conservation, Liberty Loans, Red Cross and other civilian services. A special mimeographed news letter was addressed to influential Italians.

Italian journalists were selected to tour America and report their impressions. Italians who lived in America were encouraged to write letters home, telling about the great American effort. Newspapers were induced to cooperate, pamphlets and booklets were put in print, Americans (especially of Italian origin) were sent over to speak, and motion picture reels and lantern slides were furnished in great profusion. American photographs and postcards, ribbons and buttons, posters, flags, music and exhibits were multiplied everywhere. A detachment of real, live American soldiers was brought to Italy, less for fighting than for exhibition purposes, and they aroused tremendous enthusiasm as the advance guard of America's contingent.

The dominating theme in all this was America's strenuous effort to win the War. The head of the Mission to Italy writes,

> Our only inaccuracy consisted in understating the magnitude of American preparations. We felt that since Americans had a reputation as boasters it would be better to understate than to overstate, and were greatly pleased to receive, after having been in Italy for some months, a friendly criticism from an Italian who declared that the information that we were furnishing did not reveal the full strength of America's effort.

Strenuousness in the conduct of the war is not, of itself, sufficient to arouse the enthusiasm of an ally, if there is any reason to suspect that the war aims of one ally are at cross purposes with those of another. The English were continually forced to deal with an undercurrent of suspicion in France that victory would be used to the disadvantage of France. Persistent rumours crept about that the English were not only planning to stay in Calais, as shown by the fact that they were building quarters of permanent material, but that they were chiefly instrumental in prolonging the War for the sole purpose of using French blood to drown a dangerous commercial rival. In the hard winter of 1917 Mr. Wickham Steed, of the London *Times*, was appalled to discover how much headway had been made by the insinuation that a favourable peace could be secured at any time, if England were willing to return the colonies which she had taken from Germany.

Steed seized the opportunity in one of his lectures to explain that the former colonies of Germany could never be disposed of at the arbitrary whim of Downing Street. The British Empire was no longer, strictly speaking, an Empire ; it had become a Commonwealth of Nations, whose component members had spilt their blood in these former German territories, and would never consent to permit Downing Street to use them as mere bargaining points. Steed believed that it was only by explaining the constitutional facts of the British Empire that the rumour could be squashed once and for all.[1]

Some of the lukewarmness of Italy toward American participation in the War was due to the widely circulated assertion that America had entered the War to capture the commercial supremacy of the world. The American plan

[1] See Steed, *Through Thirty Years*, II : 135.

was to loan vast sums to the impoverished Governments of Europe and, once the War terminated, to demand compensation of an unspecified, but alarming kind. This subtle campaign of insinuation and suspicion was met by a vigorous Wilsonian propaganda, which dwelt upon the disinterested and humanitarian character of America's war aims.

The French were grieved to discover that American opinion was by no means united in support of the thesis that Alsace and Lorraine should be handed over to France at the end of hostilities. The French War Mission to the United States busied itself to convert the Americans, and the French High Commissioner, M. Tardieu, strained every nerve in this direction. A few months after his arrival in May, 1917, he takes pleasure in recording,

> this state of opinion was entirely changed. I venture to believe that the activities of my co-workers and myself, the 15,000 lectures in English where young officers, with all the authority of their war record and of their wounds, presented the pitiful situation of the captive provinces, had something to do with this transformation. (He organized an Association of Alsatians and Lorrainers in America.) Thousands of huge posters, reproducing Henner's *Alsacienne* with the text of the Bordeaux protest . . . had carried the meaning and scope of our claim to every State in the Union.[1]

The process of " selling " one country to another is illustrated by the campaign to secure American support, which was waged by the friends of Lithuania in 1919. The Lithuanian National Committee retained a public relations

[1] André Tardieu, *The Truth About the Treaty*, p. 240.

counsel to conduct a campaign which was practically tantamount to encouraging an ally to accept the aims (complete
independence) desired by its minor partner.   The following
moves were made by the public relations counsel :

> He had an exhaustive study made of every conceivable
> aspect of the problem of Lithuania from its remote and
> recent history and ethnic origins to its present-day marriage
> customs and its popular recreations.   He divided his
> material into various categories, based primarily on the
> public to which it would probably make its appeal.   For
> the amateur ethnologist he provided interest and accurate
> data of the racial origins of Lithuania.   To the student of
> languages he appealed with authentic and well-written
> studies of the development of the Lithuanian language from
> its origins in Sanscrit.   He told the " sporting fan " about
> Lithuanian sports, and he told the women about Lithuanian
> clothes.   He told the jeweller about amber and provided
> the music lovers with concerts of Lithuanian music.
>
> To the senators he gave the facts about Lithuania which
> would give them basis for favourable action.   To the
> members of the House of Representatives he did likewise.
> He reflected to those communities whose crystallized
> opinions would be helpful in guiding other opinions facts
> which gave them basis for conclusions favourable to
> Lithuania.
>
> A series of events which would carry with them the
> desired implications were planned and executed.   Mass
> meetings were held in different cities ; petitions were
> drawn, signed and presented ; pilgrims made calls upon
> Senate and House of Representatives Committees.   All
> the avenues of approach to the public were utilized to
> capitalize the public interest and bring public action.   The
> mails carried statements of Lithuania's position to individ-
> uals who might be interested.   The lecture platform
> resounded to Lithuania's appeal.   Newspaper advertising
> was bought and paid for.   The radio carried the message
> of speakers to the public.   Motion pictures reached the
> patrons of moving picture houses.
>
> Little by little, and phase by phase, the public, the

Press, and the Government officials acquired a knowledge of the customs, the character, and the problem of Lithuania and the small Baltic nation that was seeking its freedom.

When the Lithuanian Information Bureau went before the Press Associations to correct inaccurate or misleading Polish news about the Lithuanian situation, it came there as representative of a group which had figured largely in American news for a number of weeks, as a result of the advice and activities of its public relations counsel. In the same way, when delegations of Americans, interested in the Lithuanian problem, appeared before the members of Congress or officials of the State Department, they came there as spokesmen for a country which was no longer ignored.[1]

This sort of propaganda needs to be supplemented by constant assertions of respect and esteem. The Allies observed one another's chief holidays. The American 4th of July was spread far and wide in Europe. American propagandists staged a great demonstration in honour of Italy's entry into the World War (May 24th). The public addresses and statements issued by the Inter-Allied War Missions consisted in fulsome phraseology which rang true in moments of profound emotional agitation.[2]

Each ally ought to re-enforce the themes of domestic propaganda at every point. They must stimulate each other to realize that their own interests are at once threatened and obstructed by the enemy. It was failure on this point that may have been partly responsible for the defection of revolutionary Russia from the ranks of the Entente. Colonel Robins was sent over to Russia to aid Colonel Thompson

[1] E. L. Bernays, *Crystallizing Public Opinion*, pp. 24–27.
[2] See F. W. Halsey (ed.), *Balfour, Viviani and Joffre; The Imperial Japanese Mission*, Washington, 1918; *America's Message to the Russian People. Addresses by the Members of the Special Diplomatic Mission of the United States to Russia in the Year* 1917, Boston, 1918; René Viviani, *La Mission Française en Amérique*, Paris, 1917.

I

of the American Red Cross, and his version of what happened in Russia is a matter of public record in the hearing conducted before a Senatorial investigating committee.   Colonel Robins went out to see what the soldiers were thinking, and when he came back, Colonel Thompson asked him :

> " Now, this thing is cutting deep, is it not—this thing that is going through Russia—this defeatist culture ? " I said : " Yes, Colonel ; and it tends to disorganize the whole Russian social fabric."   He said, " Well, what about the Allied propaganda ? "   I said : " Colonel, that is worse than nothing."   The Allied propaganda at that hour, Senator Overman, was this : Pictures and written words about how great France is, how tremendous England is, how overwhelming America is.   " We will have 20,000 airplanes on the front in a few weeks.   In a few months we will have 4,000,000 soldiers.   We will win the war in a walk."   The peasant moujik said : " Oh, is that so ? Well, if the Allies are going to win the war in a walk, we who have been fighting and working a long time will go back and see the folks at home " ; and the real effect of the Allied propaganda was to weaken the moral instead of strengthening it, if I am any judge of the facts.
>
> It was agreed among us that there was an answer that was close to the ground, and that was genuine—an effort to interpret this to revolutionary Russia, cursed by the Tsar's espousal of the Allied cause in the first instance, and by all the cross-currents that followed ; that, although it was not possible at all, I knew, to get that massed revolutionary mind to think as we thought as Allies, it was possible to get them to fight Germany to save the Revolution ; and if they served the cause, we did not care anything about what they thought, and we said, " This is the situation : We have got to interpret the holding of the front and the defeat of German militarist autocracy into terms of saving the Revolution ; and it happens to be true.   We have got to say that, if the German militarist autocracy wins, the Russian Revolution is doomed.   We have got to picture it until the average soldier and peasant sees behind the German

bayonets the barons and feudal landlords coming to take back the land ; behind the German bayonets the feudal masters of industry coming back to transmute the 8 hours and 15 roubles of the Revolution back to the 2 roubles and 12 hours of the semi-slave days before the Revolution in the factories, mills, and mines.   We have got to have them see that behind the German bayonets are the grand dukes coming to destroy their local self-governing soviets and revolutionary councils.   If we do that, we can save the situation.

In the second or third conference on this matter the question of money came up.   It was a large enterprise. " How are you going to do it ? "   Well, it was perfectly apparent that you could not do it.   There was no machinery to do it, no American or Allied bureau to do it.   The Allies shared in the common curse of the autocracy in the mind of peasant Russia.   It had to be Russian, and it had to be revolutionary.

There was in the Winter Palace at that time Madame Breshkovsky, that old and yet heroic figure, possibly the greatest revolutionary figure at that time.   Madame Breshkovsky, after 40 years of service in Russia for the Revolution, was now at the Winter Palace in Petrograd, having come back from Siberia in a triumphal journey with great celebrations, having been received in Petrograd by one of the greatest gatherings in the history of that city— this old peasant woman and revolutionist received in the great railroad station in the chamber of the Tsar, honoured by the ministers of the government, and all that sort of thing.   She was now in the Winter Palace, in the Grand Duke's suite that looked out over the Neva to Peter and Paul, where she had been three years a prisoner.   It was a dramatic, a tremendous setting.   I had known her, known her for 12 years, known her when she was in this country ; had helped her in some of her work at that time. I knew Nicholas Tchaikovsky, a thoroughly sincere and genuine revolutionist, and at that time the head of the Peasant Co-operative in Russia.

It was agreed by Col. Thompson that there should be organized a committee on civic education for free Russia. Madame Breshkovsky should be chairman of the committee ;

and as members there should be Nicholas Tchaikovsky ; Lazaroff, the Russian revolutionist, who had been head of the milk station or dairy in Switzerland, which was really an underground station for the Russian Revolution, for many years, and well known with credit through service to his country ; Gen. Neuslakovsky, the most trusted member of Kerensky's general staff, who was in active co-operation with this committee from the military angle ; and David Soskice, Kerensky's private secretary. They were to form the committee on " Civic education in Free Russia." The programme was this : " We will begin by buying some newspapers, and with other publicity we will prepare simple statements in peasant patois and in the general terms of the Russian peasant's and workingman's mind, by Russian peasants and workmen, not by intelligentsia. We will send into the ranks and into the peasant villages this new gospel of fighting German militarist autocracy ; not to serve the Allies but to save the Revolution.[1]

Colonel William B. Thompson spent one million dollars of his own money on this sort of propaganda in an effort to stave off the defection of Russia.[2]

At the first of the War the keynote of the Allied propaganda was very properly the thesis of ultimate victory against an aggressive Germany. It required all the ingenuity of the Allied representatives in Russia to bolster the Russian moral during the months of August and September when the French and British armies were recoiling before the German avalanche. The French Ambassador, writing in his diary of those days, records :

I have seen to it that these events should be presented by the Russian Press in the most suitable (and perhaps the truest) light, *i.e.*, as a temporary and methodical retire-

[1] *66th Congress, 1st Sess., Sen. Doc. No. 62.* 3 : 775 *et seq.*
[2] One of the novelties of the propaganda to keep Russia in the War was the organization of a battalion of Russian women to shame the men into fighting Germany.

ment, a prelude to a *volte-face* in the near future for the purposes of a more formidable and vigorous offensive. All the papers support this theory.[1]

He was confronted by this situation :

Financial circles in Petrograd are in continuous communication with Germany through Sweden, and all their views on the war are inspired by Berlin.

The thesis they have been expounding during the last few weeks bears a thoroughly German stamp. We must see things as they are, they say. The two groups of belligerents must realize that neither will ever succeed in vanquishing and really crushing the other. The war will inevitably end in arrangements and compromise. In that case, the sooner the better. If the hostilities continue, the Austro-Germans will organize an enormous fortified line around their present conquests, and make it impregnable. So in the future let us give up these futile offensives ; with the inviolable protection of their trenches, they will patiently wait until their disheartened adversaries moderate their demands. Thus peace will inevitably be negotiated on the basis of territorial pledges.

. . . I never fail to reply that it is our enemies' vital interest to obtain a swift decision, because, when all is said and done, their material resources are limited, while ours are practically inexhaustible. In any case the German General Staff is condemned by its theories to preserve an offensive strategy.[2]

There are circumstances in which the unity of operations is seriously prejudiced by stimulating the self-confidence of an ally. The Germans were fearful lest the Austrian and Hungarian authorities might grow too sanguine of the future and resent their subordination to the northern ally.[3]

The propaganda which is directed to disaffected groups

---

[1] Palæologue, *An Ambassador's Memoirs*, I : 103.
[2] Palæologue, as cited, II : 108.
[3] Nicolai, *Nachrichtendienst, Presse, und Volksstimmung im Weltkrieg*, 59.

inside a nation may be powerfully reinforced by inter-Allied co-operation. The Catholics of Italy were not only subjected to the appeals of certain Italian leaders who were friendly to the Allies, but from such men as Cardinal Gibbons, Cardinal Farley and Cardinal O'Connell, of the American hierarchy. The Labour groups of Italy were reached, not alone by pro-Ally leaders at home, but by a visiting selection of Radicals from abroad. The Americans brought over Alexander Howat (" the man who never lost a strike ") and John Spargo.

Inter-Allied propagandas of friendship require a reciprocal control of attitudes. Most of the friendly sentiments toward an ally are manufactured by one country among its own population. The stimulation of pro-ally emotions at home is more important than the stimulation of pro-ally sentiments abroad. The themes to employ are identical with the ones which have already been enumerated in connection with the problem of arousing an ally.

Sometimes the business of retouching the figure of an ally in the public mind is a delicate and precarious operation. Arthur Meyer frankly marvelled at the extent of the *rapprochement* between France and England, for he could remember when the children of Paris were chanting the couplet :

> Jamais, jamais en France
> L'Anglais ne règnera !¹

Sometimes a frank apology helps, as when the celebrated writer, Pierre Loti, of the French Academy, published in the *Figaro* his plea to Serbia :

> Pauvre, petite Serbie, devenue tout à coup martyre et sublime, je voudrais au moins lui ramener les quelques

¹ *Le Gaulois*, October 19, 1914.

cours français que mon dernier livre a peut-être éloignés
d'elle.[1]

The most delicate problem was how to evoke a pro-
Russian response in the ranks of the British public. For
many years the traditional menace to the Empire had been
Russia, and not Germany, and the stories of Russian
absolutism froze the blood of a nation inoculated with
parliamentarism. The success in revamping the public
attitude was indeed notable, and Basil Thompson, head of
Scotland Yard, looks back upon it rather cynically from the
vantage ground of subsequent years :

> It is strange, now, to think that in March, 1915, Russia
> was thought in England to be breathing a new inspiration
> to the West. It was said that the Crusader spirit was
> alive again, that the whole Russian nation was inspired
> with a determination to rescue Constantinople for Christiani-
> ty, and to win again the holy sepulchre ; . . . vodka was
> prohibited with the unanimous approval of the nation ;
> . . . crime had almost disappeared among the peasants. . .
> If they were successful in the war they were told that there
> would be a struggle between their religious idealism and
> their high ethical instincts and the monster of western
> materialism from which, so far, they had kept themselves
> clean. All this was honestly believed by persons who
> thought they knew Russia ; now, after a short six years,
> their voices are heard no more.[2]

When a bond of traditional friendship unites two countries,
it is simple to invoke it for emergencies.   In this style does
Gaston Riou welcome the Americans in his *Lafayette, nous
voilà !* (Paris, 1917.)

[1] August 8, 1914.
[2] *Queer People*, p. 63.   Should the exigencies of the international situation require it, this quotation can be used to cast aspersions on post-war
reaction in England.

Important as the maintenance of friendly relations between the nations fighting on one side really is, the crucial problem for the outcome of the war often is the attitude of the neutrals. The essential problem in controlling neutral attitudes is to lead the neutral to identify your enemy as his enemy and your aims as his aims.

There is an imperceptible slant in the war news, which comes from one side rather than another, which leads to the propagation of a powerful bias toward the contending nations. Almost inadvertently one comes to speak of "our victory," "the enemy retired," or "our lines held." The fact that England controlled the cables to the United States was a precious advantage in her favour. The Germans were never able to perfect their wireless service to the point of competing with the cables on a plane of equality. Less from original bias than from a subtle entanglement in the bias of the news, there appeared in certain New York papers headlines of this character, even when the Germans were pounding down through Belgium and northern France :

> BELGIUM BEATS GERMANS ; ENGLISH ARMY
>   TO AID HER.
> GERMANS LOSE THOUSANDS IN BELGIUM.
> ROUT OF GERMANS IN BELGIUM TURNED INTO
>   A SLAUGHTER.

The direct representation of the other side as an enemy of the neutrals may take a multitude of forms. As early as 1915 a book was devoted to the horrible fate of America in case Germany should win the War. In J. Bernard Walker's *America Fallen : A Sequel to the European War*, the Germans sack New York (London, 1915). This time-honoured device was employed at the time of the Franco-Prussian war to incite England against Germany. In *Blackwood's Magazine* for April, 1871, appeared an article called " The Fall of England, or the Battle of Dorking," which was reprinted as a pamphlet and sold broadcast.

The Germans found it impossible to raise the claim that Great Britain intended to attack America, since the British were obviously very much engaged in Western Europe. Instead, they insinuated that the attack upon America would come by the characteristically English method of indirection. Japan would do the will of England. What other interpretation, indeed, could there be placed upon the Anglo-Japanese Alliance ? Why is Japan

> feverishly engaged in ship building and has now under way 168,000 tons of shipping ?
> We Americans feel safe, peaceful and conceited as we sell to Europe tools with which they murder each other, and as we say to ourselves, " We are too big to be in danger."
> We would feel differently if we knew that Japan, representing all Asia, all the yellow race, had decided that the moment had arrived to make the attack, and to make both sides of the Pacific Japanese.[1]

Jefferson Jones viewed *The Fall of Tsingtau* (New York, 1915) with alarm, and the book was of some aid in arousing suspicion of the Japanese.

The heterogeneous composition of the American community lent itself to special propagandas. It was possible to arouse the Jews against the Russians, the Irish against the British, the Westerners against the Japanese, and (for some time)

---

[1] S. Ivor Stephen (Szinnyey), *Neutrality ? The Crucifixion of Public Opinion. From an American Point of View*, Chicago, 1916, p. 18. This is a repository of German propaganda themes.

the Italians against the French.   The Entente could appeal to the English, French, Scotch, Welsh, Russian, Serbian, Rumanian elements, and, after the growth of anti-Austro-Hungarian sentiment, to the South Slavs and the Czecho-Slovaks and the Poles.

The hereditary enemy of America, the *Erbfeind*, was England, and upon the anti-English chord the Germans strummed incessantly. It was England who burned Washington in 1814, and drew from Jefferson the bitter saying that

> It was reserved for England to show that Napoleon in atrocity was an infant compared to her ministers and generals.

It was, moreover, the dastardly English who stirred up the Indians to massacre the Americans who lived on the frontier during the Revolutionary War, and the War of 1812. Perfidious Albion is still trying to put something over, and Mr. O'Reilly, through the hospitable columns of the Hearst press, asked :

> Are we not being bribed to sacrifice our own best interests as well as our moral scruples, and to send arms to England, so that then she can exterminate the Germans and obliterate Germany, and possess herself of Germany's commerce and colonies ?[1]

The Central Powers were set forth as the champions of the traditional American principle of a free sea. This thesis was argued in William Bayard Hale's pamphlet, *American Rights and British Pretensions on the Seas*.[2]   The

[1] Cited in Stephen, as cited, p. 171.
[2] See also, H. L. Gordon, *The Peril of the United States;* Rudolf Cronau, *Do we need a Third War for Independence ?*

British offset this appeal by exposing the German plans to expand into South America after the War, regardless of the Monroe Doctrine, and to conquer the world for German trade, by cementing a European bloc.[1] The British likewise rose to assert that they were fighting a war of democracy versus militarism and autocracy, and they published General Bernhardi's *Germany and the Next War*, to convict the whole nation. A brilliant rationalization such as that of H. G. Wells in *Mr. Britling Sees it Through*, won a large audience in America.

Hand in hand with other plans must go the systematic vilification of the enemy. During the Franco-Prussian War the French raised a great outcry in England at the proposed bombardment of Paris, bitterly assailing the Germans for their barbarous indifference to the priceless treasures of civilization. Bismarck was quite aware of the importance of this appeal to neutral sentiment, and instructed one of his propaganda secretaries to draft an article for the Press on this theme :

> If the French wanted to preserve their monuments and collections of books and pictures from the dangers of war, they should not have surrounded them with fortifications. Besides, the French themselves did not hesitate for a moment to bombard Rome, which contained monuments of far greater value, the destruction of which would have been an irretrievable loss.[2]

When the London *Standard*, which was hostile to the Germans during the War of 1870, printed a story by the

---

[1] See André Chéradame, *The Pan-German Plot Unmasked*, New York, 1916. Mildred S. Wertheimer restored *The Pan-German League* to its proper perspective in 1924. Roland G. Usher had written a book on *Pan-Germanism* which was published in 1913, and given a renewed lease on life by the Entente sympathizers after 1914. See also his *The Winning of the War*, New York and London, 1918.

[2] Busch, *Bismarck*, I : 158. 26 September, 1870.

Duc de FitzJames, in which various Prussian abominations at Bazeilles were described, Bismarck dictated an answer to be transmitted to the English Press. He argued that the horrors of the War were not horrors of the Germans, but of the foolish stories of Prussian cruelty which frightened the peasants into deserting their homes where they would have been secure. He attacked the reliability of the Duc as witness.[1]

During the same War, the French prepared a pamphlet for circulation at home and abroad which was entitled *La Guerre comme la font les Prussiens.* Bismarck instructed Busch,

> Please write to Berlin that they should put together something of this description from our point of view, quoting all the cruelties, barbarities and breaches of the Geneva Convention committed by the French. Not too much, however, or no one will read it, and it must be done speedily.[2]

During the World War the neutrals were deluged with propaganda stuff, in which the sins of the enemy were exposed to public gaze. Besides the appeal to the general sentiment of the neutral nation, hosts of special appeals were launched. The Germans circulated an appeal to Protestants in neutral countries to rise and protest against the mistreatment of missionaries by the English. Rev. W. Stark prepared a pamphlet on *The Martyrdom of the Evangelical Missionaries in Cameroon,* 1914, (Berlin, 1914). Such damages as were inflicted in the occupied territories to churches were assigned to the Germans. The Catholics, as the chief sufferers, organized a special propaganda com-

---

[1] Busch, *Bismarck,* I: 148. 22 September, 1871.
[2] Busch, *Bismarck,* I: 406. 4 February, 1871.

mittee to work on foreign Catholic opinion. The nature of its work appears from the following list :

> René le Cholleux, *Notre Dame de Brébières ; l'Allemagne et les Alliés devant la conscience chrétienne* (pref. Mgr. Alfred Baudrillart).
> *La Guerre Allemande et le Catholicisme.*
> Raoul Narsy, *Le Supplice de Louvain.*
> *L'Éveil de l'Ame française devant l'appel aux armes.*
> L'Abbé Pasquier, *Le Protestantisme Allemand.*
> L'Abbé E. Foulon, *Arras sous les Obus.*

Mgr. Pierre Batiffol published his letter, *A un neutre catholique* in 1915, for the edification of the non-combatants. The French Protestants followed the example of their Catholic brethren, and established a committee for foreign propaganda and advertised *Nos sanctuaires dévastés.* The Italians used the same weapon in the pamphlet, *Austrian Barbarities against Italian Churches* (Florence, 1917).

This atrocity propaganda was conducted with great ability in America, particularly by the Allies. A mass meeting at Carnegie Hall in New York protested against the treatment of the Belgians, December 18th, 1916. Rector Manning presided, and there were addresses by the Hon. James M. Beck, Alton B. Parker, Elihu Root, and telegrams from Theodore Roosevelt, Joseph H. Choate, and Archbishop Ireland. An appeal from Cardinal Mercier was read, and the whole affair procured the widest publicity in the Press.

The Russian Government went so far as to address a special memorandum to neutral powers, for the purpose of protesting against the alleged slanders which the Central Powers were industriously circulating about the conduct of her troops. She likewise objected to the *Violations of Laws and Rules of Warfare, committed by German and Austro-Hungarian troops in Russia* (1915). The Germans were outmanœuvred by the British, who secured the services of the former Ambassador Bryce to serve on an atrocity commission. The protest which the Kaiser addressed to the President of the United States against the franc-tireur excesses of the Belgians proved ineffectual. They compiled a mass of material for the purpose of incriminating the Belgians, such as the *Völkerrechtswidrige Rührung des belgischen Volks-krieges,* put out by the Foreign Office, May 10th, 1915. They advertised the misdeeds of the invading Russians in East Prussia, and sharply criticized the mistreatment of German civilians and military prisoners abroad.[1] The Belgians replied officially to the charges lodged against them, but one of the best indirect replies was a study made by Fernand van Langenhove, Scientific Secretary of the Solvay Institute of Sociology at Brussels, on *The Growth of a Legend. A Study, based upon the German accounts of Francs-Tireurs and " Atrocities."* The English version of the work had a Preface by the eminent American social psychologist, J. Mark Baldwin, a diligent Francophile during the entire War.[2] With the air and method of a serious study in collective psychology the book treated the franc-tireur stories as legends.

For circulation in America the Germans prepared an appeal to race prejudice, called *Employment contrary to*

---

[1] For example, see Auswärtiges Amt., *Greueltaten russischer Truppen gegen deutsche Civil personen und deutsche Kriegsgefangene,* 1915 ; K. Jünger and Dr. H. Vaörting, *Die Behandlung der Deutschen in England, Frankreich und Russland,* Berlin, 1915.

[2] Translated by E. B. Sherlock, New York and London, 1916.

International Law of Coloured Troops upon the European Arena of War by England and France (Berlin, 1915).

Indeed, everybody took a whirl at blackguarding his enemies and whitewashing himself. All the minorities in America had their special propaganda, issuing such things as *Austro-Hungarian Judicial Crimes* (Chicago, no date), prepared by the Jugo-Slav Committee in North America. As late as 1918 the Bulgarians tried to reach the neutral world with a defence and a counter-thrust by publishing *Les Atrocités Serbes*, by M. D. Sopiansky (Lausanne, 1918). The most important feature, of course, was to secure the services of an eminent neutral to testify to his own countrymen. Mary Roberts Rinehart (*Kings, Queens and Pawns*, 1915) and scores of publicists gave their pens to the Allied cause ; fewer helped to expound the German viewpoint.

The other side is a nefarious plotter and liar, unworthy of confidence. Frederick William Wile endeavoured to expose *The German-American Plot, the record of a great failure* (London, 1915), and every idea which convenienced the plot was dubbed with the damning epithet, " Pro-German." The Germans poured out the same dark hints and insinuations about the members of the American Press and public who dared disagree with them. The *American Truth Society* wrote about the *Treason Press*, and in this indictment they meant nearly all the American Press of metropolitan standing, except Hearst and the Chicago *Tribune*. It goes without saying that ex-President Roosevelt came in for vile abuse from the German sympathizers. Everybody tried to tar the other fellow with the same stick. Rumours of propaganda and bribery fell thick and fast.

Direct appeals to neutral opinion continued all through the conflict. In 1914 James Bryce discussed the *Neutral Nations and the War*. The Germans used one of their Swiss connections to publish an exposure of *Comment l'Angleterre combat les neutres* (Zürich, 1917) ; to which the British replied in William Archer, *An die Neutralen ! Aufruf zur Geduld* (1917). Max Gaetcke discussed *Der grosse Raubkrieg und die Interessen der neutralen Mächte* (Karlsruhe, 1916), while the French contributions to this literature included Henri Hauser, *La Guerre et les Neutres. Etude sur le sentiment démocratique dans ses rapports avec la guerre européenne* (Paris, 1917), and Ernest Lémonon, *Les Alliés et les Neutres*, 1914–16 (Paris, 1917).

To the general appeals were added the special appeals. The French Federation of Schoolteachers prepared a message, *To the Schoolmistresses and Schoolmasters of all countries.* The famous *Aufruf Gelehrter Deutschen*, which came early in the War, provoked the professors abroad to feverish hyperactivity. One of the numerous replies was intended for consumption in Southern Europe and South America. A manifestation was held at the Sorbonne on the 12th of February, 1915, and the addresses which were delivered were printed under a favourite title with the French, *La civilisation latine contre la barbarie allemande.* For the sake of interesting the wage earners, an *Appeal of the Belgian Workmen to the Workmen of all Nations* appeared in London in 1916, and a year later, *The Condition of the Belgian Workmen, now Refugees in England.*

Besides the direct themes of the order hitherto enumerated neutral opinion may be reached by indirect ones. The neutral must be confident of the ultimate success of your side. Georges Hoog published his *Lettres aux neutres sur l'union sacrée*, to impress the neutrals with the solidarity of his country. Books of type of Robert Grant, *Their Spirit. Some Impressions of the English and French during the Summer of* 1916, reassure the friends of one side and affect the indifferent. The heroism and determination of a belligerent can be illustrated in military and civilian war letters, such as *War Letters from France* (edited by A. de Lapradelle and Frederick Coudert, New York and London, 1916). The pictorial medium was chosen by the Information Department of the British Foreign Office, to impress the neutrals with British strength, and the film called *Britain Prepared,* was widely circulated.[1]

The crucial importance of the foreign correspondent is alluded to by Theodore Roosevelt in his letter to Sir Edward Grey, bearing the date, January 22nd, 1915 :

> There have been fluctuations in American opinion about the war. The actions of the German Zeppelins have revived the feeling in favour of the Allies. But I believe that for a couple of months preceding this action there had been a distinct lessening of the feeling for the Allies and a growth of pro-German feeling. I do not think that this was the case among the people who were best informed, but I do think it was the case among the mass of not very well-

[1] Rear-Admiral Brownrigg says that some influence unfriendly to Great Britain caused the film to be exhibited in the United States under the title, *HOW Britain Prepared. Recollections*, p. 37. D. W. Griffith, famous director, has recently recalled the offer made to him by Bernard Shaw in 1917 to write scenarios for him. This occurred " In 1917, just after I had completed arrangements with the British Government to do some propaganda pictures." (New York *Times*, October 11th 1926.) Another of Mr. Shaw's propaganda efforts went astray when the New York *Times* divided one of his despatches and left the impression inadvertently that Shaw was dressing down the Allies. Mr. Shaw has himself related the last incident, but professes to have no recollection of the Griffith rejection.

informed people, who have little to go upon except what they read in the newspapers or see at cinematograph shows. There were several causes for this change. There has been a very striking contrast between the lavish attentions showered on American war correspondents by the German military authorities and the blank refusal to have anything whatever to do with them by the British and French Governments. Our best war correspondent on the whole, is probably Frederick Palmer. He is favourable to the Allies. But it was the Germans, and not the Allies, who did everything for him. They did not change his attitude, but they unquestionably did change the attitude of many other good men. The only real war news, written by Americans who are known to and trusted by the American public, comes from the German side ; as a result of this, the sympathizers with the cause of the Allies can hear nothing whatever about the trials and achievements of the British and French armies. These correspondents inform me that it is not the generals at the front who raise objections, but the Home Governments, and in consequence they get the chance to write for their fellow-countrymen what happens from the German side, and they are not given a chance from the side of the Allies. I do not find that the permission granted them by the Germans has interfered with the efficiency of German military operations, and it has certainly helped the Germans in American public opinion. It may be that your people do not believe that American public opinion is of sufficient value to be taken into account, but, if you think that it should be taken into account, then it is worth your while considering whether much of your censorship work and much of your refusal to allow correspondents at the front has not been a danger to your cause from the standpoint of the effect on public opinion without any corresponding military gains. I realize perfectly that it would be criminal to permit correspondents to act as they acted as late as our own Spanish War, but as a layman, I feel sure that there has been a good deal of work of this kind of which I have spoken in the way of censorship and refusing the correspondents permission to go to the front, which has not been of the slightest military service to you, and which has had a very real effect in preventing any rallying of public opinion to you.[1]

One of the most subtle and effective forms of indirect propaganda is the encouragement of everything which draws the neutral into some form of *de facto* co-operation with the belligerent. This may be done in part by playing up the instances in which a neutral citizen takes arms on behalf of one or the other belligerent. This phase of propaganda was discussed in the following letter to the London *Times*, dated December 26th, 1916, by an American partisan of the Entente. It was called " British Publicity in the United States," and read thus :

France has known how to reach the sympathy of Americans, and her publicity has been extraordinarily effective. It has been personal and it has evoked enthusiasm. It has been written to a great extent by American soldiers in the French army, each of whom is an endorsement of France. The presence of every American participant is widely advertised by the French. He is decorated wherever there is the least occasion for doing so. He is encouraged to write of his experiences. Articles and books by American soldiers of France are published by the score. Alan Seegar's Poetry of the Foreign Legion is widely known in America, and his death was as much regretted in the United States as that of Rupert Brooke in England. Robert Herrick, one of our best novelists, joined the American Ambulance with the avowed purpose of writing a series of books from the viewpoint of a participant. I was permitted to write and publish the *Note-book of an Attaché* without ever submitting it to the French censor. There are only about 500 Americans in the French army. Yet in the United States we hear something about them every day. The newspapers are full of their doings ; every item of news from them is justly considered as an endorsement of

[1] Grey, *Twenty-Five Years*, II : 150.

France. In consequence of France's shrewdly-managed publicity America is whole-heartedly pro-French.

Because Ian Hay was a participant in the War, albeit not an American one, the publication of his book in the United States, and his extended speaking tour, shared with the books and speeches of Frederick Palmer the distinction of being the only redeeming bits of British propaganda. . . . Bruce Bairnsfather's drawings and Raemaeker's cartoons, still too little known in the United States, would prove an invaluable influence to mould public opinion.[1]

Further than this, if the neutral power can be drawn into some form of non-military participation with a belligerent, his sympathies are likely to crystallize about the object of his assistance. This is the inner significance of the tremendous campaign to secure aid for Belgian widows and orphans in America, of which one memento is the pamphlet known as *The Need of the Belgians*, prepared by an illustrious galaxy of literary stars, among whom were Thomas Hardy, May Sinclair, Arnold Bennett, Will Irwin, John Galsworthy, Anthony Hope, A. W. Mason, and George Bernard Shaw. The Committee for Belgian Relief was the sponsor for this and other details of the campaign.

The Allies succeeded in forging bonds of economic interest between themselves and America, and against this the Germans waged a propaganda offensive from the start, realizing what its implications were to be for American attitudes. William Bayard Hale wrote *The Exportation of Arms and Munitions of War* in 1915, arguing that the Allies were getting most of the benefit because of the British con-

[1] Eric Fisher Wood, *The Note-book of an Intelligence Officer*, 1917, reprints his letter on page 15. See also James Mark Baldwin, *Between Two Wars*, 2 vols., Boston, 1926.

trol of the sea, and that it was tantamount to becoming a silent partner in the Entente. His booklet was published under the auspices of the *Organization of American Women for Strict Neutrality*, organized for propaganda purposes.

The German propagandists took particular care to reach out for the women on this particular issue. A memorandum of one of the conferences of the New York bureau contains these items :

> May 24th, 1915.
> All preparations are made for carrying through the project of poster advertising. The pamphlet entitled "Thou Shalt Not Kill," written by Mr. Hale, has been printed and will be sent out. Signatures to a petition to Congress collected by the ladies now number 200,000, and will in time perhaps reach 600,000. The ladies have applied for assistance in their campaign to a number of persons named by Mr. Hale. It is suggested that it be put up to the ladies to address the petition to the President and Congress, and not wait until the collection of signatures is complete before sending it to Washington, but send them, at once, in batches of about 10,000.
>
> Mr. Hale reports that Mrs. Hale is busy upon propaganda against the exportation of horses. Mr. Claussen undertakes to have a correspondingly touching scenario (story of former fire-brigade mare slaughtered in Flanders) written.[1]

Some editorials of William Randolph Hearst were collected under the title, *Let us promote the world's peace, not promote the world's warfare* in 1915. Martin Ilsen argued the illegality of the Ammunition Trade in 1915, and the *American Independence League* broadcasted a statement by Charles Nagel on the *Traffic in Arms and Ammunition*. The *National German-American Alliance* published an open letter by Dr. Charles J. Hexamer to the Committee on Foreign

[1] *Sen. Doc. 62, 1395 (Brewing and Liquor Interests, etc.).*

Relations in which these points were reiterated. *The American Truth Society* (catering to the Irish) sought to expose the *Peril of American Finance. The British Raid upon our Resources* in 1915.

As Ambassador Bernstorff has remarked, the economic question was necessarily the centre of gravity of active propaganda in America. He shrewdly comments upon the skill of the English in applying trade restriction to America. They encroached upon the freedom to trade inch and inch, and only as they stepped in to supply the market which they curtailed. Bernstorff remarks :

> It is characteristic that the declaration of cotton as unconditional contraband was made public on the very day on which the American Press was in a state of great excitement over the *Arabic* case, so that this comparatively unimportant incident filled the front pages and leading articles of the newspapers, while the extremely important economic measure was published in a place where it would hardly be noticed.[1]

The Germans formed an association of Americans to protest against the cotton contraband, but it did little good. The cleverest move of the economic propaganda of the Germans was the provoking of " Issues," which Bernstorff has defined as

> the attempt by carefully construing individual incidents to make clear to public opinion the fundamental injustice of the English encroachments and their far-reaching consequences in practice. The most important case in this direction is that of the *Wilhelmina*. According to the prevailing principles of international law, foodstuffs were only conditional contraband. They might be imported into Germany if they were intended for the exclusive use of

[1] *My Three Years in America*, p. 89.

the civil population. As, however, England succeeded in restraining the exporters from any attempt to consign foodstuffs to Germany, especially as, in view of the enormous supplies that were being forwarded to our enemies, they had little interest in such shipment, the question never reached a clear issue. Herr Albert, therefore, induced an American firm to ship foodstuffs for the civil population of Germany on the American steamer *Wilhelmina*, bound for Hamburg, by himself undertaking the whole risk from behind the scenes (Albert was the German purchasing agent in America).

This scheme went on the rocks because the English, after capturing the ship, declared a blockade, and the decision ceased to matter. It was one of the " Issue " boats that put up a problem to the British which Ambassador Walter Hines Page was able to solve. The *Dacia*, a ship of former German ownership, which had transferred to American registry on the outbreak of war, was outfitted with crew, flag and cotton by Mr. E. N. Breitung, of Marquette, Michigan, and, after great advertisement, sailed for Germany. A terrific row would have broken out if the British captured the ship, and Page's inspiration was to allow a French warship to capture it. This went through on schedule and not a chirp was raised in America.[1]

Neutrals may eventually be drawn into the war by direct instigation. The outside propagandist may circulate such pronouncements as those of Roosevelt, who favoured the Allies, and they may encourage the activity of the war party. In Italy, the pro-Ally sentiment was whipped to the exploding point by d'Annunzio. The story is told thus by Thomas Nelson Page, American Ambassador to Italy, 1913 to 1919.

[1] The story is told in Page's *Life and Letters*, I : 394.

It had for some time been contemplated to unveil a statue to Garibaldi and " the Thousand " at Quarto, the little port near Genoa from which they had sailed on the 5th of May, fifty-five years before, for the wresting of the Sicilians from a foreign yoke and the uniting them to the kingdom of Italy. Great preparations were made for the celebration of the anniversary of what was one of the most inspiring events in the history of Italy.

The Cabinet was to attend the ceremony, and it presently became known that the King and Queen would also attend. The conviction spread throughout Italy that the occasion would be availed of to announce Italy's decision to take her place with the Forces of Liberty battling in France and declare war. All Italy was on the *qui vive*. Then, suddenly, two days before the event was to take place, the announcement came that, after all, owing to the gravity of the moment, neither the King nor the Cabinet would attend the unveiling. . .

The absence of the King and the Cabinet from the celebration at Quarto may have given it a somewhat different trend, but certainly not one less violent. The orator of the occasion, Gabriel d'Annunzio, the poet and novelist, who had come from France for the purpose, delivered with telling effect an address which was rather a lyrical rhapsody on Italian liberty and aspiration than an historical address. It fell on ears attuned to receive it, and was, in fact, a firebrand stuck into a magazine charged and ready for the explosion. That night the streets of Genoa were choked with the crowds that apotheosized Garibaldi and the orator, d'Annunzio, and clamoured for war. After this it was a continued progression—nothing could stop it. . .

The orator of Quarto came to Rome in a sort of triumphal procession, and for days spoke in a species of lyric frenzy, from hotel balconies or in theatres to excited crowds who followed him into a state of exaltation. On the 14th he spoke in the Constanza Opera House, which was heavily guarded, all approaches being picketed, by a strong force of police and soldiers, including an extra force of cavalry to preserve order and prevent demonstrations before the Government offices and the Embassies of the Central

Empires. The overflow demonstrants, left outside of the auditorium, resisted all efforts to disperse them, building barricades and tearing down a rear wall around an open lot adjoining the Opera House to use as missiles against the soldiers should the latter be too firm in attempting to clear the streets.[1]

When the state of neutral sentiment seems to be ebbing steadily away from the belligerent toward whom it is hoped to direct it, the propagandist may retire to certain last lines of defence. The Germans in the United States did what they could to encourage pacifist sentiment. The American League to Limit Armaments had been organized in 1914, by sincere pacifists who hoped to keep America out of the European maelstrom. This later developed into the American Union against Militarism, one of whose offshoots subsequently became the National Civil Liberties Bureau. The American Union Against Militarism organized the Collegiate Anti-Militarism League, and co-operated with numerous Peace Unions and Christian Socialist Fellowship organizations. The American Neutral Conference Committee was an emergency group which had the objective indicated by its name. The Emergency Peace Federation came to an early end, as did the Conference Committee. The Germans, of course, got such aid and comfort as they could from the existence of such societies and played the peace theme heavily as 1917 approached.

A dangerous idea—from the standpoint of the Allies—which the Germans propagated in America was that the Allies were the stumbling block to peace. The British were genuinely exercised by the progress of the peace drive of the Germans and Sir Edward Grey confesses that the German

[1] *Italy and the World War*, 209 *et seq.*

effort to cast the onus of continuing the War upon the Entente, was one of the most effective moves which they made.[1]

It may be possible to stir up trouble between two neutrals and thus tie the hands of the neutral. Such a purpose appears in the rather amusing story of a German feature film named " Patria." This was a serial photoplay which was released weekly in two-reel episodes for a span of ten weeks. It was made under the direction of Whartons, in upper New York, for the International Film Service Corporation, a Hearst-owned film distributing company, later re-incorporated as the International Film Service Company (Incorporated). It was made in 1916, and cost about $90,000. Mrs. Vernon Castle was the star. When it began to appear, it purported to emphasize the necessity for preparedness. By the time the first episodes were ready, the country was already launched upon a preparedness programme, leaving its anti-Japanese and anti-Mexican features as the only live ones. The picture shows the great effort of Japan to conquer America with the aid of the Mexicans. A Japanese noble, at the head of the secret service of the Emperor of Japan, was the chief villain. Japanese troops invaded California, committing horrible atrocities. The picture was first shown in New York on the 9th January, 1917. The *New York American* and other Hearst papers ran the story serially from week to week. When the anti-Japanese element had to be suppressed, the Japanese names and characters were supplanted by Mexican names and inscriptions. But in the film, they were still

[1] Grey, II : 118.

wearing Japanese uniforms.[1] At the last moment, it was thus converted into an effort to inflame two neutrals.

The *Chicago Tribune* once cited an admission in the *Neueste Nachrichten* of Leipzig, that Germany could look with complacency upon strained relations between the United States and Mexico, because, while digesting this hard nut, Jonathan must cease to be John Bull's willing servant.

The *Tribune* properly observed that

> If the United States had to devote all its energies to an enterprise such as the subjugation of Mexico, there would be less American ammunition going abroad.[2]

The famous Henry Ford pamphlets on *The War Record of the Chicago Tribune* reproduce this editorial side by side with an editorial on the twenty-first of the same month, in which the *Tribune* said that it preferred a campaign in Mexico to a campaign in Europe.

> If we win in a war against Mexico, we know what we get out of it—a secure continent.   And it is practically impossible for us to lose.

> If we finally win in a war against Germany, what do we win ?   Blessed if we know. " The overthrow of German militarism " will be the glib answer.   Yes, and the substitution of some other—Russia's, perhaps, or Japan's.

> However, though Fate offers us a golden apple in Mexico and bitter fruit in Flanders, Mr. Wilson, being for " Humanity " rather than for America, wishes us to taste the bitter one.   He probably will have his wish.

The outcome of such policy as that proposed by the *Tribune* would have been so favourable to the Central Powers, that statements of this kind were very properly

[1] See the *Sen. Doc.* 62, (*Brewing and Liquor Interests, etc.*) 1675.
[2] April 4, 1916.

circulated by the agents and friends of Germany in America. This does not, of course, imply that those who made such assertions were themselves pro-German.

When a belligerent country has a larger contingency of its former nationals in a neutral land, it may, in an emergency, seek to draw or drive these elements into active work in its behalf. Von der Goltz, a captured German agent, wrote a book on *My Adventures as a German Secret Agent in* 1917, which credits the German propagandists with an exceedingly ingenious scheme.

> *It was planned so to discredit the German-Americans that the hostility of their fellow-citizens would force them back into the arms of the German Government.*
> I happen to know that during the first two years of the war many of the stories about German attempts upon Canada, about German-American complicity in various plots, *emanated* from the offices of Captain von Papen and his military associates . . . Germany wanted to give the world convincing proof that all peoples of German descent were solidly supporting her. It was for this reason that reports of impossible German activities were set ·afloat —rumours of Germans massing in the Maine woods, of aeroplane flights over Canada. And since many anti-German papers had been indiscreet enough to attack the German-Americans as disloyal, the German agents used and fomented these attacks for their own purposes.
> But Germany overreached herself. Emboldened by the apparent success of their schemes, her principal agents, von Papen, Boy-Ed, and von Rintelen (who had begun his work in January, 1915), became careless, so far as secrecy was concerned, and so audacious in their plans that they betrayed themselves, perhaps intentionally, as a final demonstration of their power. The results you know. In so far as the disclosure of their activities tended further to implicate the German-Americans, they did harm. But by these very disclosures the eyes of many German-Americans were opened to the true nature of the influences

to which they had been subjected, and through that fact the worst element of the German propaganda in America received its death blow.[1]

The statement which von der Goltz made is not corroborated by any other evidence, and the testimony of a professional spy is always subject to the most justifiable suspicion. There is some reason to believe that this may have been fabricated for the purpose of instigating the German-Americans against a German Government which had so cynically attempted to betray them (to this purpose the last paragraph quoted seems to be directed). But there is no denying the fact that there are circumstances in which just such strategy as that imputed by von der Goltz to his superiors could be successful.

The control of inter-Ally sentiment is partly a problem of maintaining a reciprocal cordiality, and the problem of stimulating friendly relations between a belligerent and a neutral has its bivalent aspects. What is said about the neutrals and about the war in a belligerent country tends to be translated or read in a neutral country. Thus Italian susceptibilities were wounded during the critical days of 1915 by the statement of a French public man that Italy was waiting "to fly to the succour of the victor." Belligerent opinion must be supervised and managed in the interest of neutral friendship.

Ambassador W. H. Page notes that

> The Cabinet has directed the Censor to suppress, as far as he can with prudence, comment which is unfavourable to the United States. He has taken this action because

---

[1] Condensed from pages 223-233.

the public feeling against the administration is constantly increasing.[1]

Bismarck flew into a rage when a communiqué was put out by the German military authorities in 1871 saying that some shells had struck the famous Luxembourg Gardens in Paris. He demanded to have àll the subsequent communiqués submitted to him, so that the material which might be turned against Germany abroad could be deleted.[2] Bismarck put the damper on editorial criticism in Germany of the purveying of coal to the French fleet by the British, on the theory that such railing would merely handicap diplomatic arrangements.[3]   His chief was a level-headed old gentleman who felt the importance of neutral opinion, and Bismarck often had his way, even against the military people.[4]

Our discussion so far has had to do principally with the themes which bear upon the preservation of friendship. Let us now review in summary from some of the methods which were employed by the chief competitors for the favour of America. The German methods have become public knowledge through the Senatorial inquiry conducted in 1918–1919, and writings of Ambassador Bernstorff and others. The title of the hearings is itself a triumph of

[1] *Life and Letters*, II : 51 (February 15, 1915).
[2] Busch, *Bismarck*, I : 341.
[3] Busch, *Bismarck*, I : 42.
[4] Kaiser Wilhelm I. made an interesting note on the margin of a document dated May 16th, 1875 ; " Um glückliche Kriege zu führen, muss dem Angreifenden die Sympathie aller edelgesinnten Menschen u. Länder zur Seite stehen, und dem, der ungerecht den Krieg zuträgt, die öffentliche Stimme den Stein werfen. Dies war das Geheimnis des Enthusiasmus in Deutschland 1870 ! Wer ungerechtfertigt zu den Waffen greift, wird die öffenliche Stimme gegen sich haben, er wird keinen Alliierten finden, keine *neutres bienveillants*, ja überhaupt wohl keine Neutralen, wohl aber Gegner finden."

insinuation. It was " Brewing and Liquor Interests and German Bolshevik Propaganda," and was reported in three husky volumes. The hearings did not begin until September 27th, 1918, and did not figure heavily in the War propaganda. A hearing which was conducted in February and April of 1918, dealt with the National German-American Alliance.[1] Three birds were killed at one stone by these hearings : the brewers, the Germans, and the Bolsheviks. The Anti-Saloon League, the Department of Justice, the Military Intelligence and the Naval Intelligence were active in pressing the investigations.

Dr. Dernburg, former Secretary of State for the Colonies, was sent to this country at the outbreak of the War to float a German loan. The American Government warned against lending money to either side, and it was impossible to produce satisfactory results. Dr. Dernburg was also an agent for the German Red Cross and began to collect funds for this work. He also undertook to explain the German version of the War to the American public, and set up a Press Bureau in New York. Opinions differ as to whether he came over here to do this, or whether he found that it was difficult to return to Germany and evolved this to keep him occupied. He had the assistance at the New York Bureau of M. B. Claussen of the Hamburg-Amerika line, and after the entry of Japan into the War the interpreter of the Consulate-General in Yokohama joined the staff. Daily bulletins of the German Information Service were issued, and

---

[1] The hearings were before the sub-committee of the Committee on the Judiciary. The most important report is the three-volume work known as Senate Document 62, 65th Congress, 2nd Session, 1919. " And Bolshevik " propaganda does not appear in the title to volume 1.

then the activity of the bureau was extended to the preparation of pamphlets. For these efforts the services of William Bayard Hale were secured. War-pictures and film-propaganda were later added. Dr. Mechlenburg and Herr Plage were held up in America on their way from Japan and placed their services at the disposal of Dr. Dernburg. Dr. Dernburg had the assistance of a committee which he selected, consisting of Albert, Gerhardt, Fuehr and a few American journalists and business men. They conferred once or twice a month on propaganda policy. Dr. Dernburg stayed in this country until after the Lusitania incident, when he made a public speech at Cleveland, justifying the sinking of the boat on the theory that it carried arms. Public indignation ran so high that a sacrifice was demanded, and Dernburg was the sacrificial ram. He went home. Ambassador Bernstorff tried thereafter to keep the Germans from agitating too openly in the country, preferring to work through American citizens.

The Germans had the warm co-operation of the German-American Alliance, which was well organized in the German strongholds over the nation—St. Louis, Chicago, Cincinnati, Milwaukee. There were numberless German social clubs and societies. The Kriegsbund was composed of those who had served in the German army. There were several veterans' posts of the War of 1870. The Geneva Society was a peculiar organization of German waiters. The Turner Societies and all sorts of benevolent organizations were thriving in every German district.

The Lutheran Church was a strong asset of the Germans, for there were 6,000 congregations in the United States, whose communicants numbered some three million. Often their services were kept up in German, and many of their preachers had received training in Germany.

The Germans appealed to all nationalities with a grievance against the Allies. The American Truth Society was a vehicle for stirring up the Irish. The Jews had an ineradicable antipathy toward the Tsaristic system, and many of them sided with the Germans. Their Press frequently had such items as the following :

> It is impossible to be a comrade of Nicholas and not be a hooligan. In the days of Beaconsfield, when England was far from Russia, no massacres of Jews were made, not on the poor, and not on the rich. To-day, when England is an ally of Nicholas, she must do as Nicholas does, she must make massacres, she must preach against the Jews.

> When the war broke out, I immediately enlisted (in the French army), but I was astonished on my arrival at the camp at Lyons to see that I, together with many other Jews, was placed in a legion which was composed of criminals only. From all sides we were insulted. We were given cold black coffee and dry bread, and when we protested we were told that we were dirty Jews, and we came only to eat and nothing else. I refused to eat and got sick. When I applied to the sergeant to send me to the hospital, he began to beat me, etc.[1]

Concerning the efforts of the Germans to win the negroes, and to foment discord inside the country over the race question, Captain Lester testified to the committee :

> A separate department was maintained in the Albert bureau for the handling of American race problems, the principal among which was the negro question.

[1] Clippings from *Wahrheit* (New York). Sen. Doc. 62, 1825, *et seq.*

The bureau obtained through newspaper agencies and exchanges and from these so-called clipping bureaux records of every lynching in the United States, and every attack by coloured men upon a white person, or every news item which showed the alleged oppression of the coloured race.

These were formed into propaganda articles, and were forwarded to the editors of established newspapers, that is, white newspapers, and also to the editors of coloured newspapers.

The field work was conducted by a man by the name of Von Reiswitz, formerly a consul, I understand, at one time at Chicago.

His headquarters, if you may say that he had any headquarters, was in and about New Orleans, and all of the negro propaganda work was conducted from Mexico by Von Eckhardt. I say all of it in the sense that the directing head was in Mexico. The men used for the negro propaganda work were Mexicans and half-breeds, and men that were brought to Mexico City and instructed and sent across the border ; and the wave of negro propaganda work went from the Mexican border east, and embraced the States, principally, of Texas, Louisiana, Arkansas, Mississippi, Alabama, Georgia ; and States such as North and South Carolina and Tennessee were really on the outskirts of the movement.

The propaganda was directed to stir up trouble continuously between the whites and the blacks of any nature and description. That was the first item.

The attempt was also made to win the coloured race to the cause of Germany by innumerable arguments. We have information that the propaganda took this form : That the negro leaders, who were subsidized or attempted to be subsidized, in various local communities and by letters—I do not mean the big leaders of the negro race, but small men scattered here and there—told the negroes that in Germany the blacks were equal to the whites ; that in Europe they had no colour line. They exhibited statements, presumed to be authentic, to this effect, and argued with them that, if Germany won the war, the rights of the coloured people in the South would be equal to those of the whites. That was the principal argument. They played continuously upon lynchings.[1]

The Germans sought to touch every foreign language group which might be suborned by controlling the American Association of Foreign Language Newspapers.

The German University League was started in 1915, to unite all who had attended a German university. The purpose was " to co-operate with every effort, to strengthen the regard for the Germans and for their aims and ideals and to secure for them fair play and proper appreciation." Among those who were officers or trustees are to be found the names of von Klenze, William R. Shepherd (Columbia), Carl L. Schurz, von Mach, and many other distinguished academic and public men. Meetings were held and papers read and distributed. The co-operation of visiting professors, such as Moritz J. Bonn, was secured. This was a direct channel of communication between the intellectuals of Germany and America.[2]

The Germans were active in trying to reach the professionally trained people in the country. Nagel's pamphlet on American neutrality was circulated to 50,000 lawyers through the American Truth Society.[3]

The women were appealed to through the League of American Women for Strict Neutrality, which was founded in Baltimore. The wage-earners received special attention through the Labour's National Peace Council (1915). They were often very close to the brewing interests, for the latter were very much alarmed at the impending movement for

[1] *Sen. Doc.* 62, (*Brewing and Liquor Interests, etc.*) 1785.
[2] For documents, see *Sen. Doc.* 62, 1372 *et seq*.
[3] *Sen. Doc.* 62, 1424.

Prohibition, and German propaganda agents sometimes took advantage of the anxiety of the brewers to make propaganda by offering to organize such a movement and turning it into a pro-German drive.

All manner of appeals to the public at large were made through all available channels. Books upon every phase of the War were put out under the auspices of the Dernburg-Albert Bureau, and the circulation of every book, beneficial to the German cause, was facilitated. A short selection of these books follows :

> *England or Germany*, Frank Harris.
> *Hindenburg's March into London*, L. G. Redmond-Howard, author of the *Life of John Redmond*.
> *Peace and America*, Hugo Münsterberg, Harvard University.
> *America's Relations to the Great War*, John W. Burgess, Columbia University.
> *The Making of Modern Germany*, Ferdinand Schevill, The University of Chicago.
> *England*, Eduard Meyer, The University of Berlin.
> *Belgium and Germany*, *A Dutch View*, Dr. J. H. Labberton.
> *Justice in War Time*, Bertrand Russell.
> *Behind the Scenes of Warring Germany*, Edward Lyell Fox.[1]

The *New York Mail* was purchased for the sake of reaching a metropolitan audience, and supplying a newspaper which could be quoted. Cartoons, pamphlets and photographs without number were employed, and distributed through steamship company offices.[2]

Moving pictures were sent to America in which German soldiers were shown busily feeding Belgian and French

---

[1] A fuller list is given in *Sen. Doc.* 62, 1410 *et seq.*
[2] Additional information about the German system appears in Lewis Melville, "German Propaganda Societies," *Quarterly Review*, 230 (1918) : 70–88.

children. There were such captions as " Barbs feeding the hungry," " Do Barbarians look like this ? "

The head of the British propaganda in America has conveniently summarized his methods.[1]

> Practically since the day war broke out between England and the Central Powers I became responsible for American publicity. I need hardly say that the scope of my department was very extensive, and its activities widely ranged. Among the activities was a weekly report to the British Cabinet on the state of American opinion, and constant touch with the permanent correspondents of American newspapers in England. I also frequently arranged for important public men in England to act for us by interviews in American newspapers ; and among these distinguished people were Mr. Lloyd George (the present Prime Minister), Viscount Grey, Mr. Balfour, Mr. Bonar Law, the Archbishop of Canterbury, Sir Edward Carson, Lord Robert Cecil, Mr. Walter Runciman (the Lord Chancellor), Mr. Austen Chamberlain, Lord Cromer, Will Crooks, Lord Curzon, Lord Gladstone, Lord Haldane, Mr. Henry James, Mr. John Redmond, Mr. Selfridge, Mr. Zangwill, Mrs. Humphrey Ward, and fully a hundred others.
>
> Among other things we supplied three hundred and sixty newspapers in the smaller states of the United States with an English newspaper, which gives weekly reviews and comment on the affairs of the war. We established connection with the man in the street through cinema pictures of the Army and Navy, as well as through interviews, articles, pamphlets, etc. ; and by letters in reply to individual American critics, which were printed in the chief newspaper of the State in which they lived, and were copied in newspapers of other and neighbouring States. We advertised and stimulated many people to write articles. We utilised the friendly services and assistance of confidential friends ; we had reports from important Americans constantly, and established association by personal correspondence with influential and eminent people of every

[1] Sir Gilbert Parker, " The United States and the War," *Harper's Magazine*, 136 (1918) ; 521–531. Extract.

profession in the United States, beginning with the university and college presidents, professors, and scientific men, and running through all the ranges of population. We asked our friends and correspondents to arrange for speeches, debates and lectures by American citizens, but we did not encourage Britishers to go to America and preach the doctrine of entrance into the war. Besides an immense private correspondence with individuals, we had our documents and literature sent to great numbers of public libraries, Y.M.C.A. societies, universities, colleges, historical societies, clubs and newspapers.

It is hardly necessary to say that the work was one of extreme difficulty and delicacy, but I was fortunate in having a wide acquaintance in the United States, and in knowing that a great many people had read my books and were not prejudiced against me. . . .

. . . it should be remembered that the Society of Pilgrims, whose work of international unity cannot be over-estimated, has played a part in promoting understanding between the two peoples, and the establishment of the American Officers' Club in Lord Leconfield's house in London, with H.R.H. the Duke of Connaught as President, has done, and is doing, immense good. It should also be remembered that it was the Pilgrims' Society, under the fine chairmanship of Mr. Harry Brittain, which took charge of the Hon. James M. Beck when he visited England in 1916, and gave him so good a chance to do great work for the cause of unity between the two nations. I am glad and proud to think that I had something to do with these arrangements, which resulted in the Pilgrims taking Mr. Beck into their charge.[1]

The chief emphasis in Sir Gilbert Parker's succinct account of his own methods is upon the use of persons as channels of influence. Influence spread from business man to business

---

[1] The British have not publicly estimated the amount of money which they spent on American as distinguished from other types of propaganda. They spent one hundred and fifty thousand dollars (£31,360 4s.) in the last four months of the War to break the German moral and to accomplish other propaganda objects.

man, from journalist to journalist, from professor to professor, from worker to worker. Behind the scenes, and behind the news and pictures and speeches, there flows a mighty stream of personal influencing. The War was more debated in private than in public. The doubters were won by friendship or flattery, logic or shame, to fuse their enthusiasm in the rising wave of Allied sentiment. A side-light on the method is contained in a letter from Sir Edward Grey to Theodore Roosevelt, dated September 10th, 1914:

> My dear Roosevelt,--J. M. Barrie and A. E. W. Mason, some of whose books you have no doubt read, are going to the U.S. Their object is, as I understand, not to make speeches or give lectures, but to meet people, particularly those connected with Universities, and explain the British case as regards this war and our view of the issues involved.[1]

When a lance was broken in public for the British cause, it was done by an American and not by a foreigner. There were no obnoxiously evident Britishers as there were Dernburgs in America. It was the social lobby, the personal conversation, and the casual brush which forged the strongest chain between America and Britain. All countries found that an effective carrier of propaganda for their cause in America was the titled foreigner who said nothing whatever for the public prints, but who talked privately and casually of the War. The sheer radiation of aristocratic distinction was enough to warm the cockles of many a staunch Republican heart, and to evoke enthusiasm for the country which could produce such dignity, elegance and affability. The wife of an important newspaper proprietor was hostess

---

[1] Grey, *Twenty-Five Years*, II : 143.

to a Count ; the wife of a Senator evened the social score by
countering with a Duke. A Marquis, Earl or Baron was
dealt hither and thither in this diverting social game. All
this was a standing joke among sophisticated Europeans,
who subtly played upon the ambitions of numerous hostesses
in New York, Philadelphia, Boston, Washington and
Chicago.

The most important personality in propaganda among
neutrals or allies usually is the official representative at
the capital. What type of man should he be and what
technique should he exploit ? No more brilliant success has
ever been scored than that of Benjamin Franklin at Paris
during the War of Independence. A Frenchman, M. Francis
P. Renaut, describes him in these words :

> (Franklin) arrived preceded by a certain reputation ;
> he was able not only to save his admirers from disillusion,
> but to kindle their enthusiasm. For some he was scientist
> who had captured the lightning, for others the genial
> philosopher, for others the enemy of tyranny and the ardent
> defender of public liberty ; for all, he was the simple man of
> nature, the patriarch, the father of a family who unostenta-
> tiously exemplified the common virtues. And in a time
> when the words of Rousseau were lodged in every cultivated
> mind, who could fail to be moved by the spectacle of a
> venerable old gentleman coming to defend his country,
> supported on the arm of one of his grandchildren (William
> Temple Franklin). The politician scarcely appeared in
> this life, of which the smallest details captivated the
> Parisians ; the residence at Passy with its easy access, the
> visits to Court without ceremony, the philosophical
> conversations, the relations with Voltaire and the
> physiocrats.[1]

---

[1] *La politique de propaganda des Américains durant la Guerre d'Indépen-
dance*, I : 52.

The key to Franklin was expressed by implication in the last sentence : he was a non-political personality, and the lustre of his person spread to all his affiliations.

An example of a dubious selection is that of the Hon. Elihu Root as head of the American Mission to Russia. There was no question about his technical eminence as a student and administrator of international affairs, but the situation was such that he was open to attack in revolutionary Russia. As Colonel Robins testified :

> You may know that he had attacked at one time in this country a very important public person, and you may know that, as a result of that attack, editorials, the most brilliant possible of their kind, had been published for successive weeks, accompanied by cartoons, speaking of Mr. Root as the jackal of privilege, as the watchdog of Wall Street, and all that sort of thing. They had been run in the public Press. Probably the German agents in America, immediately upon his appointment, gathered these up and sent them over, and they appeared in pamphlets in Russia, translated into Russian, with the cartoons and the words changed to Russian synonyms, so that even friendly papers said, " How is it possible that the great democratic President should send over to Russia to help make the world safe for democracy—to revolutionary Russia—the man who has spent most of his time, according to what we hear, in trying to make America safe for plutocracy ? "[1]

If this general analysis of the technique of preserving friendship is correct, it goes to show that the chief theme of inter-allied propaganda is strenuous exertion in the common cause, and that every supporting thesis of propaganda should be sustained and reinforced. The handling of the neutral boils down to the problem of leading the neutral to identify

---

[1] *Sen. Doc. 62, (Brewing and Liquor Interests, etc.)* 3 : 819.

his own interests with your own in defeating the enemy. Aside from general representations of the enemy as threatening, obstructive, and despicable, and of one's own nation as protective, helpful and upright, there must be some confidence in ultimate success. The most astute means of drawing in neutral sympathy is to draw the neutral into overt co-operation in some form. When all else fails, an appeal to pacifism and an effort to instigate trouble with another neutral may avoid active hostility. Among all the means to be exploited, the use of personal influencing is peculiarly important, as is the practice that in general neutrals should be addressed by neutrals.

CHAPTER VII

DEMORALIZING THE ENEMY

It is possible to employ propaganda as a weapon of direct attack against the moral of the enemy by seeking to break up or divert the hatred of the enemy from a belligerent.

To a certain degree this can be accomplished by a campaign of simple counter-stimulation. The *Gazette des Ardennes* was published by the Germans for the consumption of the Frenchman who lived within the occupied area, and the various themes capable of employment in demoralizing the enemy were used at one time or another within its columns. The *Gazette* was exhaustively examined by Professor Marchand during the War for the purpose of establishing, if possible, a direct parallel between its attitudes and those of the *Bonnet Rouge* of Paris. His report, which was part of the evidence against the latter journal in the famous trial of 1917, has since been published as *L'offensive des Allemands, en France, pendant la guerre.* It is made up of assorted extracts from the two papers in question, and represents by far the best systematic study of one phase of War propaganda yet made. The references in this section will be to this compilation, supplemented by other material. In most cases the citations have been checked against the original.

The *Gazette* denied outright that Germany had ever

plotted to attack France, and deplored the propaganda of misrepresentation against Germany. M. Léon Daudet and M. Clemenceau have the " spionnitis," when they imagine that Germany had sown France with a vast army of secret agents before or since the War.[1]

The *Gazette* defended its Kaiser and military men from the alleged calumny of the Allies. William the Second has always been recognized as a powerful influence for peace. It was he who saved Europe from war over Morocco. His pacific spirit has repeatedly been acknowledged by such men as J. Holland Rose, the eminent English historian, by Marcel Sembat, the Frenchman of letters and Socialist-patriot, and by right-thinking people everywhere. He is conscientious, peace-loving, kindly, gentle in his family relations, able in his leadership, and altogether generous in his impulses.[2]

All the stories about German barbarities are poisonous lies. The German soldiers in the army of occupation in northern France are kind to children. A picture in the *Gazette* for December 1st, 1915, shows a German soldier in the act of feeding a little French child who is perched affectionately on his knee.[3] The children cherish fond memories of "l'oncle Fritz."[4] Letters from Frenchmen in the occupied territory and from French prisoners in the hands of the Germans, were published to prove the kindly and considerate character of the German forces of occupation.[5] The irrepressible German

[1] *Gazette*, July 2, 1917, citing an item from the *Frankfurter Zeitung* Marchand, p. 97.

[2] *Gazette*, 17 November, 1917. Marchand, p. 143.

[3] Reproduced opposite page 145 in Hansi and Tonnelet, *A Travers les Lignes Ennemies*.

[4] *Gazette*, 13 August, 1916. Marchand, p. 25.

[5] *Gazette*, Same.

love of music, religion and morality has manifested itself wherever German soldiers are found.

The tales of wholesale atrocity and wilful destruction are malicious generalizations from a few regrettable individual instances, which happen in every army, but less often in the disciplined German army than elsewhere. The necessities of war, as everyone knows, may require acts which are not essential in the quiet times of peace, but it is absurd to distort the facts into a wholesale denunciation of an entire nation.[1] Many of the churches which the Germans are supposed to have destroyed were never destroyed, and many of them were illegitimately used by the enemy.

The examples which have been cited so far illustrate defence by denial. Another form of defence, that of admission accompanied by justification, is illustrated by the handling of the U-Boat question. The *Gazette* explained over and over again that the submarine was nothing more nor less than a reply to the infamous and illegal British blockade.

While no form of stimulation should be neglected, and the application of counter-suggestion has a certain effect, its efficacy is by no means comparable to the influence of a skilful propaganda of diversion. To undermine the active hatred of the enemy for its present antagonist, his anger must be distracted to a new and independent object, beside which his present antagonist ceases to matter. This is a very difficult operation, and it is always advisable to carry through a work of preparation for the purpose of undermining some of the varieties of resistance which hamper the success of such a manœuvre.

[1] *Gazette*, 7 June, 1916. Marchand, p. 190.

Patriotism is a powerful prop to belligerent ardour, and anti-patriotic propaganda has some chance to succeed with those elements in the nation who begin to recover their peace time ideology after the war has worn on awhile.   The *Gazette* published certain items which deplored the tendency of patriotism to lead a country into needless slaughter.[1] Patriotism which preaches hate is immoral, and the poisoning of men's minds is nothing less than criminal.[2]   The war spirit should be avoided, since there is no doubt of its irreligious and unethical character.[3]

Another sustaining force against which sapping operations must be directed is the confidence of the people in their government's honesty.   If a suspicion can be engendered against the propaganda of the government and the war party, a potent weapon of disintegration is created.   The Germans complained that they were the victims of systematic vilification by ignorant pedagogues, irresponsible politicians, and lying newsmongers.

But the keynote in the preliminary spade work is the unceasing refrain : Your cause is hopeless.   Your blood is spilt in vain.   Now the heads of the French propaganda very properly criticised the early English propaganda for boasting of the size of the Allied armies during the early stages of the War, when the Germans occupied Belgium and northern France.   It was only when things settled down to a stalemate or worse, and when disappointment was general, that such propaganda became effective.   When the British took the offensive in 1918, in a military sense, they simul-

[1] 23 September, 1916.   Marchand, p. 85.
[2] *Gazette*, 9 January, 1916.   Marchand, p. 15.
[3] *Gazette*, 3 July, 1917. Marchand, p. 27.

taneously sowed the German trenches with maps upon which their gains were plainly marked. They recalled the false hopes which the German leaders had held out to the people and the army. They circulated an alleged statement in a German newspaper which lamented that

> A few weeks ago it appeared as if our armies were very near their goal, the defeat of the enemy force, and peace. But what a change !

Forebodings were disseminated. A card was spread over the German trenches with the legend :

> To-day we are in retreat. Next year we shall be destroyed.

When the German generals gave public evidence of their alarm at the incursions of Allied propaganda in 1918, the Allied pamphleteers interpreted this to the Germans as a sign that their leaders wanted to keep the truth from them. A rumour that the German Government was at last disposed to make peace was circulated as another evidence of weakness.

The Americans, who entered the field of direct propaganda against Germany, and especially the German army, spent most of their energy advertising the news of America's strength. Little leaflets with a row of soldiers, whose size varied with the monthly increase in the number of American soldiers, were distributed over the German lines. 1,900,000 Americans are now in France, said the card, and more than ten times as many stand ready in America. The extent of German casualties and tonnage losses was emphasized. That they were short of food and raw materials was insinuated by such means as circulating the report that another smuggler had been arrested in a German city.

Tracts with such questions as these were distributed far and wide :

> Will you ever again be as strong as you were in July, 1918 ?
>
> Will your opponents grow daily stronger or weaker ?
>
> Have your grievous losses suffered in 1918 brought you the victorious peace which your leaders promised you ?
>
> Have you still a final hope of victory ?
>
> Do you want to give up your life in a hopeless cause ?[1]

Another theme of first-rate importance when it is in juxtaposition to the foregoing is the privations to which the soldier and his family at home are subjected. Stories of want and misery at home were featured in a special French propaganda sheet, which was prepared for use among German soldiers, the *Briefe aus Deutschland*. In the brilliant attack upon Italian moral, which preceded the disaster of Caporetto in 1917, the Italian soldiers were sent appeals, ostensibly from home, beseeching them to lay down their arms and return to their families.

The joys of home were subtly suggested by the French editors of *Die Feldpost* (another sheet for the German troops). They celebrated the Christmas season of 1915 by recalling all the simple pleasures of Christmas at home with the family in peace.[2] The amusements of civilian life were featured in the propaganda literature for the sake of intensifying war weariness.

---

[1] Heber Blankenhorn describes the American campaign in *My Adventures in Propaganda*.

[2] Hansi and Tonnelet, Figure 4, opposite p. 24.

Another means of stressing want and privation is to circulate, as the Americans did, something which suggests the relative affluence and luxury of the enemy. A card, which was an exact reproduction of the official German field postal card, said :

> Write the address of your family upon this card, and if you are captured by the Americans, give it to the first officer who questions you. He will make it his business to forward it in order that your family may be reassured concerning your situation.
> (On the reverse) :
> Do not worry about me. The war is over for me. I have good food. The American Army gives its prisoners the same food as its own soldiers : Beef, white bread, potatoes, beans, prunes, coffee, butter, tobacco, etc.[1]

This was no new wrinkle in propaganda technique, for it is recorded that handbills were circulated among the British troops on Bunker Hill, offering them seven dollars a month, fresh provisions in plenty, health, freedom, ease, affluence, and a good farm, should they desert and join the American Army.[2]

All the preparatory or auxiliary themes outlined so far are supposed to facilitate the task of substituting new hates for old. The next step is to concentrate upon the particular object of animosity about which it is hoped to polarize the sentiment of the enemy. One of the possible alternatives is to transfer suspicion and hatred to an ally.

The German propaganda did what it could to disinter the ancient animosity of the French for the English. France,

---

[1] Reproduced in Blankenhorn, p. 78.
[2] C. K. Bolton, *The Private Soldier under Washington, p.* 90. Cited by Salmon, *The Newspaper and the Historian*, 340.

they said, is the cat's-paw of the English. The English have been exceedingly backward in their war preparations, as Winston Churchill has recently acknowledged.[1] Their game is to let France bleed for them. Indeed, they are taking pains to establish themselves in permanent buildings at Calais, and any student of history knows how long it took to dislodge England the last time she had her clutches on Calais.

The truth, declared the Germans, is that, far from threatening you, we are willing to join you in a common crusade against England, who has conspired with some of your meanest politicians to use your blood to crush our trade competition. We will gladly free you from the machinations of England, and help you to expand your colonial domain at the British expense. Between us we can dominate Europe, and to dominate Europe is to dominate the world. At the same time, we can emancipate you from Russia, whose Tsar is using France to enable him to grab Constantinople.[2]

The Allies, in their turn, strained every muscle to drive a wedge between Austria-Hungary and Germany. Rumours that the Dual Monarchy was negotiating a separate peace, were circulated among the German soldiers on the Western Front, for the purpose of stirring up hatred against Austria, and of demonstrating the hopelessness of the cause for which they had suffered so much. The report that the Austrians and Hungarians had plenty of food provoked considerable animosity in Germany, where the food restrictions were

---

[1] *Gazette*, 7 September, 1916. Marchand, p. 49
[2] *Gazette*, 26 April, 1917. Marchand, p. 47.

severe. The Austrians, for their part, were taunted as the slaves of Prussia, and wheedled by the possibility of territorial compensations at the expense of Germany, should they change sides.

An ally is not the only possible object of diversion. The government and the governing caste may serve just as well. If the ruling person, clique or class can be made sufficiently obnoxious, Revolution comes, and in Revolution there is little remaining capacity for active hatred of the external enemy.

During the last war every belligerent took a hand in the perilous business of fomenting dissension and revolution abroad, reckless of the possible repercussions of a successful revolt. There is reason to believe that, as early as 1915, the Germans were attempting to foster the collapse of Russia, by placing revolutionary reading matter in the hands of those Russian prisoners who might eventually return to Russia through exchange or release.[1] The famous episode of the sealed car, which contained Lenin and forty men, happened in 1917.

The Allies set about quite consciously to uproot the Kaiser and the Imperial system in Germany. One of the leaflets which the French scattered over Germany contained a picture of the Kaiser and his husky sons, unscathed by war ; on the opposite side stood many rows of wooden crosses, to mark the final resting places of his loyal German subjects.[2] Another leaflet showed the Kaiser and his general

---

[1] A Russian who was permitted to visit some of these prison camps through the Red Cross arrangements made this the subject of a complaint.
[2] Reproduced in Hansi and Tonnelet, p. 136.

staff, sitting about a table, conversing genially and drinking beer ; the reverse pictures an explosion in a front-line trench, where many bodies are being ripped to pieces.[1]

German Republicans who lived abroad were drafted or volunteered to discuss the responsibility of the Kaiser for the War. After the collapse of the great offensive in the spring of 1918 the Wilsonian propaganda in Germany reached its apex. His speeches were strewn far and wide, and they were successful in creating the impression that a Republican Germany would receive a soft peace from the western democracies. Care was taken to print all the passages of Wilson's speeches which had been suppressed in Germany in red ink.[2]

The British tried to suggest the imminence of revolutionary disturbances in Germany by means of news items, which told about secret precautions recently taken in Berlin, where a G.H.Q. order had just directed certain measures to be taken for the suppression of strikes. Every Socialist meeting which was suppressed received considerable publicity on the Western Front. The following item is a particularly subtle effort to carry the idea of revolution. It is in the form of a despatch from Stockholm :

> The German Minister in Stockholm has requested the Swedish Foreign Office to seize the copy of the *New York Herald Magazine of the War* of the 14th of July because it publishes on the front page a photograph of the German Emperor, underneath which are the words :—" What shall we do with the Kaiser after the War ? " The Minister of

---

[1] Reproduced in Hansi and Tonnelet, p. 160.
[2] See Hansi and Tonnelet, p. 152.

Justice is said to have ordered the copies in question to be seized.[1]

Although the Germans were finally bested in the game, they tried strenuously to demoralize the Allies through Revolution. Through the *Gazette* and every other channel open to them they endeavoured to hang the responsibility of the War upon Poincaré and his clique. This was the group, they said, whose insane lust for revenge led them to carry on illicit negotiations with military and diplomatic circles in Belgium, to finance strategic railways in Russia, when they ought to have been providing for social welfare at home, to refuse to thwart the propaganda for Pan-Slavism, and to violate Belgian neutrality before Germany entered the War.

The Germans came into possession of a crushing reply to the professions of international idealism with which the Allies filled the air. They gave as much publicity as their limited resources would permit to the secret treaties which the Allied powers had made. The idealistic Allies had carved up the world among themselves. Russia was promised Constantinople. Great Britain got the neutral zone north of its sphere of influence in Persia. The Italians got the Trentino and Trieste, plus the Slavic territories of Gorizi, Gradisca, Istria, Dalmatia and Valona. They were promised 200,000 Germans who lived in the Brenner Pass region and who had been Austrian subjects since the fourteenth century. The important ports of the Adriatic (except Fiume) fell into their hands outright, or were neutralized.

---

[1] This and similar examples are given in Campbell, *Secrets of Crewe House*.

They secured the Greek Dodekanese Islands, some provinces in Asia Minor, and promises of colonies in Africa. Rumania was given territories inhabited by Serbs, Hungarians, Ruthenians and other Slavic nationalities. France gave Russia a free hand in Poland in return for a free hand on the western front in reference to Alsace-Lorraine, the Saar, and the left bank of the Rhine. Besides all this, the Turkish Empire and the colonies of Germany were sliced up and parcelled out.

The revelation of these treaties not only created inter-Allied troubles, because the secret treaties revealed that the Allies had made contradictory promises to some of the weaker powers, but it had an immediate influence on the moral of Labour. The revelation of Allied duplicity produced the repercussions which have been referred to before.[1]

The Germans carried their attack upon national unity very far. They sought to arouse the wives at home by calling attention to the alarming extent to which prostitution was practised at the front. Dr. Graux records that, as early as July 1915, anonymous pamphlets were distributed in France, elaborating this theme.[2]

No effort was spared to arouse the soldiers at the front against the supposed excesses of politicians, profiteers and officers behind the lines. The *Gazette* for November 5th, 1916, alluded to the wives of soldiers left at home who find duty too burdensome to bear. The French Government was known to be responsible for importing the black inhabitants of Morocco into the War, and the *Gazette* took

---

[1] Page 62.
[2] Graux, *Les Fausses Nouvelles*, II : 151.

occasion to publish a letter which contained the remark
that

> Those dirty Moroccans have left offsprings right and
> left, like the Annamite.[1]

The French reproduced and circulated a cartoon from
Simplicissimus; in which a German schoolmaster asked an
emaciated pupil why anyone is called a poor sinner, who is
condemned to severe punishment. The reply was:

> " Because a rich sinner is never punished severely."[2]

The authorities encouraged fraternization between the
Austrian and the Italian troops before the Caporetto affair,
carefully using for that purpose some Austrian Communists,
who had been infected by Communism or Socialism on the
Russian front. Sometimes German pacifists were permitted
to travel abroad, although the most rigorous limitations
were placed on their agitation at home.

The Germans appealed to every possible cleavage in the
French nation, seeking to instigate party versus party,
farmers versus urbanites, provincials versus Parisians,
workers versus employers, the army versus the nation, the
army versus the government, and the legislature versus the
executive.[3]

We have spoken of anti-Ally and anti-Government propaganda, but some attention must be given to a third
important possibility, anti-State propaganda. The late
War proved how effective the instigation of secession may be,
when the belligerent is a heterogeneous State. The Allies

---

[1] *Gazette,* April 29, 1917.   [2] See Hansi and Tonnelet, p. 28.
[3] Marchand. Section II.

began to talk about self-determination early in the War. The Tsar announced that he proposed to grant autonomy to a united Poland on the 16th of August, 1914. By the spring of 1916 the astronomer-aviator, Stefanik, offered to drop Czech proclamations by Masaryk over the lines of the Austrian Army, opposite the Italians.[1]

The Russians had dropped some gold coins with the Czechish national castle minted on one side inside the lines by aeroplane, but it was not until after the Declaration of Corfu in July, 1917, that the propaganda offensive against the Dual Monarchy began to inflict its greatest damage. According to this declaration, Pashitch and Trumbitch, " the authorized representatives of the Serbs, Croats and Slovenes," recognized the desire of our people " to constitute itself in an independent national state "; adopted as its name " the Kingdom of the Serbs, Croats and Slovenes "; provided for the unification of its flag and Crown, but also for the free use of special Serb, Croat and Slovene flags and emblems ; for the freedom of the Orthodox, Roman Catholic and Mussulman creed ; declared that the Adriatic must be " a free and open sea," and that " the Kingdom will include all territory compactly inhabited by our people and cannot be mutilated without attaint to the vital interests of the community."

The policy of partitioning Austria-Hungary was opposed, even at this comparatively late date, by numerous elements among the Allies. The *New Europe*, which was launched in October 19th, 1916, by Seton-Watson, Masaryk, Steed and certain others, tried to overcome the reluctance of the

---

[1] Steed, *Through Thirty Years*, II : 102.

British Government to come out boldly for the policy of partition. The Allied governments were embarrassed by the deal into which they had entered to bring Italy into the War in 1915, at which time the aspirations of the Southern Slavs were not definitely formulated. The Italians had been offered guarantees which were utterly incompatible with the unity of the Southern Slavs, and the Italians were disposed to hang fast to the advantages of the treaties. They preferred annexations to the problematical friendship of an aggrandized Serbia, and they feared that a dismembered Austria would join Germany. Wickham Steed, of the London *Times*, an active member of the pro-Serbian propaganda group, credits the Jewish financial houses with wishing to maintain the German-Jewish financial system, which had formed the economic framework of Pan-Germanism, and with wishing to strengthen every element of opposition to the break-up of Austria-Hungary. The Roman Catholic hierarchy was likewise against the total submergence of the largest remaining Roman policy in Europe. British society cherished a soft spot for the Austrians because their homes were so well kept, their shooting so good, and their urbanity so unruffled.[1]

Indeed, it was not until after the disaster of Caporetto in October, 1917, that the Slavs and the Italians were able to agree, and to enable the Allied propaganda to assume its final proportions. Even then, it was not until the " Pact of Rome " of March, 1918, that the way was entirely cleared for one of the greatest propaganda feats of the War, the Congress of Oppressed Hapsburg Nationalities, which met at

[1] Steed, II : 129.

Rome in April. On October 26th, 1918, there was a convention in Philadelphia of twelve nationalities, who were determined upon securing liberty from their former rulers. The presiding officer was Professor Masaryk, who was the president of the Czecho-Slovak National Council, which had been recognized by the Allied governments. Most of the Press spoke of the gathering in Independence Hall as a Czecho-Slovak Convention because of Masaryk's prominence and the tremendous impression which had been made upon the public mind by the Czecho-Slovak Legion in Russia, and the Division of Czecho-Slovak troops in France. All the delegates to the Convention solemnly signed a Declaration of Independence, and the event was widely heralded in America and Europe.[1]

Another brilliant stroke on the part of Allied propaganda was the encouragement of Zionism. In November, 1917, Mr. Balfour, then Foreign Secretary of Great Britain, committed the British government to the establishment of a Jewish National Home in Palestine. This gave the material for an able appeal to the Jews in Germany and, incidentally, increased the interest of American Jewry in the War. General Ludendorff regarded the Balfour Declaration as the cleverest thing done by the Allies in the nature of war propaganda, and lamented the fact that Germany had not thought of it first.

The efforts made by the Central Powers to instigate secession fell flat. As early as the spring of 1915 the Austrians tried to dissolve Russia. The French Ambassador

---

[1] For an account of the proceedings, see the agitation journals. The *Czecho-Slovak Review* for November, 1918, summarizes it briefly.

was told by Goremykin, President of the Council, on the
10th of April, 1915, that

> Austria is making great efforts to create a national move-
> ment among the Ukrainians.   Surely you know that there
> is a society for the Liberation of the Ukraine in Vienna ?
> It publishes pamphlets and maps in Switzerland.   I get
> them, and they certainly reveal very intense propaganda
> activity.[1]

Germany tried to stir up the Irish against the English
and to precipitate trouble in Northern Africa, Egypt and
India.   They tried to split Belgium by encouraging the
" Walloon movement," but to little avail.

Several movements which were, in effect, a *reductio ad
absurdum* of the principle of self-determination were begun
during the War.   One of them grew in the fertile brain of a
member of the Austrian Press service.   He chanced to be in
occupied Italian territory and overheard a conversation
which he could not quite make out.   He discovered that
it was a local speech known as Friul, spoken in a few villages
in Udine Province.   He wrote an article demanding self-
determination for the users of Friul, and precipitated quite
an angry Press campaign in Italy.

A large element in propaganda against the enemy is the
invention of ways and means for the transmission of suggestions to the enemy.   It is proposed to deal with some
of the more specialized appliances which were used for this
purpose in the last War rather than to touch upon them in
the section which is devoted to the general consideration of
tactical matters.

---

[1] Palæologue, *An Ambassador's Memoirs*, I : 327.

Efforts were first made by the belligerents to penetrate behind the lines of their opponents by means of insertions in the neutral Press. Newspapers were purchased in Switzerland and other neutral countries for this purpose. Almost simultaneously the belligerents began to invent ways and means of direct transmission.

The French began to publish a regular periodical in October, 1915, for dissemination among the soldiers of their opponents. The periodical was variously known as *Die Feldpost, Kriegsblätter für das deutsche Volk*, and *Das freie deutsche Wort*. Books and occasional pamphlets were copiously employed. A tiny edition of *J'accuse* was sent far and wide, for the purpose of preaching German responsibility for the War. By the same method various books were published from the pens of Dr. Herman Fernau, Dr. Muehlen, Prince Lichnowsky and others. Several fervent brochures, prepared by Dr. Hermann Rosemeier, who until his flight in September, 1914, had edited the *Morgenpost* of Berlin, were distributed.[1]

Die Kriegsfackel was put out occasionally for the sole purpose of discussing the question of war guilt.[2] *Briefe aus Deutschland* and *Grüsse an die Heimat* were also published irregularly. The former was devoted to letters and news items upon internal conditions in Germany, and the latter was made up of letters from German prisoners who testified about their excellent treatment in France. The French forged a number of the *Strassburger Post*, a famous organ of

[1] *Die Vorgeschichte des Krieges; Deutsches Volk, wach' auf!* See Hansi and Tonnelet, opposite p. 56.
[2] See Hansi and Tonnelet, opposite p. 38.

Germanization, on the 29th of August, 1916, and on the 16th October, 1917. This was principally intended to encourage the pro-French elements inside Alsace and Lorraine, and was full of sparkling satire upon German administration. The famous yarn about the British intention to occupy Calais was dealt with as follows :

> We are able to confirm this almost incredible news (that the French have leased Calais to the English for 99 years). Our correspondent has interviewed a French officer of high rank (adjutant) in Switzerland, originally from the vicinity of Beaucaire, who, in tears, and with every mark of dejection, confessed that he had himself *seen* the city of Calais and the English government conclude the contract. The rental was fixed at 255,000 pounds sterling per month ; it is payable in advance on the first of each month. Upon receiving this amount, the Mayor of Calais divides it among the inhabitants of the city. All expenses for light and street cleaning, together with an obligation to sprinkle sand on the sidewalks in case of a freeze are assumed by the renter ; the owner pays for repairs. Either party may terminate the contract at will upon nine months' notice.— Behold the depths to which France has fallen in humiliating herself before the perfidious Albion ! If the citizens of Calais imagine that the intrepid German Michel intends to deliver them from the clutches of the English, that nation of shopkeepers, they are deluding themselves. . . . We have already tried it once, and we will most assuredly not undertake it again.[1]

The French also forged a number of the *Frankfurter Zeitung* in July, 1917. They copied and parodied the leaflets which were used for war loan propaganda in Germany. Republican propaganda which was written by Siegfried Balder and a troupe of others was sent over the lines.

---

[1] Hansi and Tonnelet, p. 60.

Special pamphlets were devoted to justifying the French claim to Alsace and Lorraine.

In addition to these efforts, the French published *La Voix du Pays* for distribution among the occupants of the invaded territories and of Alsace and Lorraine. Special appeals were addressed to the Bavarians in the hope of stirring up the South against the North. The French tried to send as much of their propaganda as possible through the Swiss postal service into Germany. They used a Swiss publishing house to prepare material which they smuggled over the border. One clever agent sold preserves to Germany and stuffed the cartons with Allied propaganda stuff.

In 1916 the British War Office[1] created a branch of the Directorate of Military Intelligence known as M.I.7.b., the new staff establishing *Le Courrier de l'Air* for the purpose of reassuring the inhabitants of the invaded territory that the cause was not lost. Copies of the paper even reached the interior of Germany, where they aroused the fury of the German authorities. This paper was published uninterruptedly from April 6th, 1917, until January 25th, 1918. Its publication was suspended for a time, as a result of an order issued by the German military command to try the occupants of any aeroplane which carried " seditious literature " by court-martial, and to inflict severe penalties upon them. This threat was followed by an example of its execution, and the *Courrier* was suspended until a new mode of dissemination could be perfected. Publication was resumed March 7th, 1918.

---

[1] Major C. J. C. Street, " Propaganda Behind the Lines." *Cornhill Magazine*, 3rd Series, 47 (1919) : 488–499.

The development of better methods of distribution is traced by Major Street in these pages :

There is no intrinsic difficulty in scattering pieces of paper any more than there is in scattering pieces of steel, but the desired destination of the two forms of missile varies, as does the effect they are intended to produce. A shell, to secure its maximum effect, should burst in the centre of a group of men ; propaganda leaflets, on the contrary, should be dispersed as widely as possible, and then should avoid the highly disciplined group, and should arrive within the grasp of the lonely sentry, free from the influence of his compatriots, and with nothing else to divert his thoughts. The group would probably treat a leaflet as a joke, the isolated man would read it through sheer boredom, and would possibly be induced to believe that there was something in its argument. And once propaganda has secured even the vaguest mistrust of the doctrines that it combats, its task is more than half accomplished.

Both the Allied Powers and the Central Empires experimented with propaganda projectiles, using the trench mortar as their means of projection. The idea was, in most cases, to construct a bomb with a small bursting charge, which should, upon its arrival over the opposing lines, release a shower of pamphlets upon the heads of an astonished enemy. But the system had its obvious drawbacks. A trench mortar has always been an unpopular weapon, credited with the effect of incurring retaliation more than outweighing the damage it may possibly produce. Further, the most susceptible might well be expected to resent a shower of words hurled at him by so direct a method or, if not to resent it, at all events to ridicule it as rather too obvious a *ruse de guerre*. There is something inconsistent about an army that makes life unbearable with " flying pigs " one moment, and the next sends out, through the mouths of the very same weapons, a flood of literature proclaiming that all men are brothers, or some other pacific doctrine. It was not long before the trench mortar, as a projector of propaganda, was abandoned in favour of the aeroplane.

This later weapon seemed at first to have every qualification for the purpose. It could scatter innumerable leaflets from any convenient height, and, owing to the length of time taken by them in falling, their arrival had no visible connection with its flight. Far more effect would naturally be produced by a leaflet blowing into a trench from nowhere in particular than from one obviously hurled by a lethal engine. Further, the aeroplane had a far greater penetration, could scatter its propaganda over rest-billets and railheads as well as over the trenches themselves. The advantages of this were twofold : the leaflets could be found and picked up over a far greater area, and men some way back from the line had more leisure and inclination to ponder their contents. But, on the other hand there were many other calls upon the aeroplanes available. It was argued with a considerable show of reason that if a plane could be sent upon a flight over hostile territory it would be better employed dropping bombs than propaganda. Some went so far as to say that the best propaganda that could be dropped over the enemy were bombs and plenty of them, a contention that was correct as regards the Rhine towns and incorrect as regards London. At all events, it was felt that the aeroplane was too valuable a fighting machine proper to be employed as a disseminator of leaflets.

The next idea was the employment of observation balloons, which were to carry a supply of pamphlets to be thrown overboard when the wind was blowing towards the enemy lines. Apart from the fact that the occupants of the balloon were usually too busy with their proper function of observation to worry much about casting packets of paper into space, the observation balloon had many disadvantages. A more ingenious and elaborate development of the observation balloon scheme was a revival of the man-lifting kite. When the wind was favourable, the kite was flown from some suitable spot, and a " follower," carrying a bundle of leaflets, caused to travel up the taut string of the kite. The " follower " was fitted with an automatic release, which functioned at a predetermined height, allowed the leaflets to fly away, and the " follower " to fall to the ground again ready for recharging. When the contrivance did not jamb, it was a very entertaining toy to play with.

It was not until late in 1916 that the free balloon was seriously considered as a vehicle of propaganda. The idea had always been obvious ; load a balloon with the leaflets it was intended to distribute, send it up with a fa'vourable wind, and there you were. The difficulty lay in predicting within a thousand miles or so where the balloon would come down. It was not until the science of meteorology, urgently impelled by the needs of the Artillery, made its marvellous war-time developments, that balloons could be used scientifically. " Meteor," in the shape of the various meteorological experts attached to the forces, eventually became able to gauge the velocity and direction of the wind at practically any height in any given locality. The rest was simple, so soon as a simple and reliable release had been evolved. You took your balloon to a given spot, say, ten miles behind the lines, you knew your balloon would rise to, say, six thousand feet, and travel at that height until its burden was released. " Meteor " gave the velocity of the wind at twenty miles an hour, south-west, at that height and place. Forty miles from the balloon position, and bearing north-east, was an enemy concentration camp. Load your balloon with the required type of propaganda leaflet, set your release to act in rather less than two hours, to allow of drift of the leaflets when falling, and there you were.

. . . The balloons were made of paper, " doped " with a preparation to render them hydrogen tight.

As equipped for service in France, a propaganda balloon section consisted of a couple of three-ton lorries for the conveyance of the hydrogen cylinders, balloons, and leaflets, with the necessary personnel of officer and a few men. Certain stations were selected, such that some desirable target could be reached with any direction of wind from north round by west to south. . . .

The means of attachment was the solution of the whole problem of the use of balloons, and was as simple as it was ingenious. A length of the orange-coloured woven tinder, sold at every tobacconist's for use in pipe-lighters, was taken, and one end of it fixed to the balloon. The sheaves of leaflets were strung on cotton tags, as used for binding papers in Government offices. The end of each tag was driven through the length of tinder at calculated distances from the free end.   The rate of burning of the tinder was ascertained by experiment, and found to be, say, one inch in five minutes.   If the target were twenty miles an hour, the balloon would be over the target in forty minutes.   The tags would then be inserted at close intervals from six to ten inches from the end of the tinder.

Just as the balloon was released, the end of the tinder was held against a lighted cigarette, and commenced to burn.

The Allies had the wind at their backs during most of the summer and autumn of 1918, when their propaganda attained its greatest proportions, and material was distributed over a zone, 150 miles deep, behind the German lines.   By August they had achieved a distribution of 100,000 leaflets a day, which meant that between four and five million leaflets were sent over monthly.

The Allies solved the problem of distribution much better than the Germans were able to do.   One of the finest strokes of German propaganda was the publication of the captured list in the *Gazette des Ardennes*.   This made it possible for the people in the occupied territory to have a valid excuse to read a paper which was obviously pro-German.

A clandestine Press service was built up to supply the Belgians with news of the Entente world, and was an important influence alike in the stimulation of their own moral, and in permeating the nearest German populations.[1]

This review of the problem of demoralizing the enemy seems to show that the principal theme is the impossibility of victory, and that a discouraged nation may turn against an ally, or its own governing class, and lose by the secession of minority nationalities.

---

[1] See, for the story of *La libre Belgique*, Jean Massart, *The Secret Press of Belgium.*

CHAPTER VIII

SUCCESSFUL propaganda depends upon the adroit use of means under favourable conditions. A means is anything which the propagandist can manipulate ; a condition is anything to which he must adapt. A propagandist can alter the organization of his activities, modify the streams of suggestion which he releases, and substitute one device of communication for another, but he must adjust himself to traditional prejudices, to certain objective facts of international life, and to the general tension level of the community. Both the conditions and the methods of propaganda have been mentioned explicitly or by implication in the course of the present study, and the time has come to draw them together in more systematic form.

The achievements of propaganda are affected by the traditional prejudices of the nation and of each constituent group. The French had the advantage of a great historic friendship with America, a heritage of the gratitude which the struggling colonists felt for aid of the French in the Revolution. The Germans counted upon the sympathy of their former nationals, and of the Irish-Jewish blocs. The British could rely upon a very deep and pervasive community of feeling, which was so general that it was frequently ignored in the presence of more spectacular and less profound attitudes.

Propagandists are always likely to run foul of some deeply imbedded prejudice. Thus the Germans seized upon the alleged franc-tireur excesses of the Belgian people to justify their own acts to the world and to the German public. But when the Prussians began to circulate tales of Catholic priests who urged their parishioners to kill the invader with every means in their command, a cross-current was set up at home. The Catholics arose to contradict the rumours. The Catholics had organized a *Zentralauskunftstelle der katholischen Presse* in 1900. This was revamped into the *Rechtschutzstelle für die katholische Geistlichkeit* at Frankfurt in 1913. In 1906 another service was set up at Cologne, bearing the name *Priesterverein Pax für das katholische Deutschland*. Both services began to cast insinuations and contradictions upon the Prussian versions of Catholic atrocities in Belgium, and these were snapped up abroad and used by the Allies to discredit the German tales about Belgium.[1]

Such prejudices continually circumscribed the propagandist. His freedom is further restricted by the network of connections between nations. The British held the cable communications between America and Europe in the hollow of their hands, and this had far-reaching results. The Germans tried in vain to offset such a handicap by exploiting the wireless, but with mediocre success. Anyone who knew the history of American foreign attitudes could have pre-

[1] See Albert Hellwig, " Zur Psychologie des Belgischen Franktireur-krieges," *Preuss. Jahrb.*, Bd. 174 : 361–388.

dicted in 1914 that the British viewpoint stood an excellent chance of infecting America, for American public opinion has often been a cockle-shell, floating helplessly and unconsciously in the wake of the British man-of-war.   After the Civil War the American nation was a warm friend of Russia and bought " Seward's ice box " as a gift of gratitude for the Tsar's moral support during the conflict.   In the supervening years, America had few direct contacts with Russia, but American friendship passed over into active hostility. The explanation is very simple : America was fed on the British Press and Britain was in conflict with Russia.

There are objective similarities and differences in social customs and institutions between two nations, and these cannot be waved aside.   After all is said and done, it was true that Britain, France and Belgium were more democratic than Germany in their basic political institutions, and that Americans spoke English and read English, and not German.   Americans knew Shakespeare and not Goethe, and they thought the Battle of Waterloo was won by the Duke of Wellington, and not by Blücher.   The basic patterns of American life were more English than German.[1]

There are often interpenetrations of population which make it difficult to control sentiment at will.   The customs and habits and competitive power of various immigrant groups in America influenced the American attitude and the attitude of their countries of origin.   Many of the Russians who returned home when the Revolution came, carried back tales of reeking tenements and twelve-hour

[1] For an able exposition of these points see the booklet by Professor Moritz Bonn, *Amerika als Feind*.

shifts in the steel mills. When the American propagandists undertook to extol the virtues of American democracy, some embarrassing questions were always forthcoming from the audience.

One form of population interpenetration, which is particularly important in war, is the quartering of invaders upon the inhabitants of a conquered territory. A foreign military occupation produces all sorts of friction between the authorities and the inhabitants, and the distressing incidents which abound in war are particularly common then. The Germans occupied Belgium and were embarrassed by compromising collisions with the civilians. The Allies were able to make tremendous play with everything that happened and a great deal that did not ; the Germans could only retort by repeating the horrors of the Russian occupation of Eastern Prussia, which was too far away to arouse the sympathy and pity of the Americans.

There may be important connecting links of an economic character between two countries. It is generally recognized as a principle of international politics that when a country has loaned money to another it is likely to come to the aid of its debtor, should a third party threaten its ability to pay. The Americans who loaned their money to the Allies during the period of American neutrality may have advanced it out of sentimental preference for the Allied cause (the House of Morgan was English in origin and affiliation), but once tied to the Allies, the cords of sympathy were strengthened by bonds of gold. The sequel confirms the axiom that the creditor is bound to the debtor.

During the war-time the relative military strength of the

contesting parties is a decisive point. Great movements of retreat cannot be concealed for long, and prolonged humiliation spreads the seeds of discord and defeatism. The German propagandists could invent no new hope to replace the disillusionment of midsummer, 1918 ; the appeal to arms had exhausted their credit, and destroyed the simple faith of the masses. Lord Grey has written some sage words about how easy it is to exaggerate the rôle of diplomacy in war-time, and what he says applies to propaganda, which is one of the tools of diplomacy. The pivotal front is the military front.

> Even the battle of the Marne was, to outside opinion, rather the saving of Paris than a great victory, an arrest of the German advance rather than a turning of the tide in favour of the latter. Then followed the first battle of Ypres, in which the Franco-British line was brought near to another catastrophe. In 1915 there were no Allied successes of magnitude sufficient to counteract the deplorable impression made by the huge Russian disasters. In 1916 the Germans failed at Verdun, but the French suffered heavily, and the year was rather one of German failure than of Allied success, except the Brusiloff offensive. This brought the Rumanians in. Even the gaps in the Austrian line made by Brusiloff were completely stopped in a short time. The task of Allied diplomacy in Europe during the war was indeed uphill and thankless work.[1]

The preceding paragraphs have enumerated some of the connecting links which bind nations together and which condition the success of propaganda. These are, for the most part, quite tangible things which anyone can see on close inspection : the communication network, similarities and differences in customs and institutions, interpenetration of

[1] Lord Grey, *Twenty-Five Years*, II : 165.

population, economic ties, relative military power. We now come to a limiting factor which is unquestionably present, but which is neither simple to describe nor to explain : the tension level.

By the tension level is meant that condition of adaption or mal-adaption, which is variously described as public anxiety, nervousness, irritability, unrest, discontent or strain. The propagandist who deals with a community when its tension level is high, finds that a reservoir of explosive energy can be touched off by the same small match which would normally ignite a bonfire.

Some day it will undoubtedly be possible to connect the fundamental biological and psychological processes with this phenomenon, but to-day the field is a battleground of rival conjectures. Every school of psychological thought seems to agree, however, that war is a type of influence, which has vast capacities for releasing repressed impulses, and for allowing their external manifestations in direct form. There is thus a general consensus that the propagandist is able to count upon very primitive and powerful allies in mobilizing his subjects for war-time hatred of the enemy. The possibility also exists that there are physiological or psychological types which respond more readily than others to the bellicose stimuli circulated by the propagandist.[1]

It may be that further research will confirm the hypothesis of Clark Wissler, that there are special situations in the

---

[1] For the concept of the tension level in individual psychology, see the masterly essay by Pierre Janet in the *Traité de psychologie* (edited by Dumas), Tome I. Applications of the notion of liberated repressions to war will be found in the books of such widely separated psychologists as Ernest Jones and George Patrick (*Essays in Psycho-analysis* and *The Psychology of Relaxation*).

cultural life of a group in which definite psychological dispositions lead toward expansion. This anthropologist writes :

> when a group comes into a new solution to one of its important culture problems, it becomes zealous to spread that idea abroad, and is moved to embark upon an era of conquest to force the recognition of its merits.[1]

He also says that the extension of the material culture zone beyond the zone of political control, is likely to produce irritations which lead to an attempt to enlarge the political zone to coincide.[2]

Certainly, there is reason for believing that the propagandist who works upon an industrialized people, is dealing with a more tense and mobile population than that which inhabits an agrarian state. Industrialism has apparently increased the danger from those secret mines which are laid by repression, for it has introduced both the monotony of machine tending, and the excitement of much secondary stimulation. The rhythm and clang of exacting machinery is no less characteristic of the industrial way of life, than the blazing array of billboards, window displays, movies, vaudevilles, and newspapers, which convey abundant and baffling possibilities of personal realization. The stage is set, and

> a coarse patriotism, fed by the wildest rumours and the most violent appeals to hate and the animal lust of blood, passes by quick contagion through the crowded life of the cities, and recommends itself everywhere by the satisfaction it affords to the sensational cravings. It is less the savage yearning for personal participation in the fray than the feeling of a neurotic imagination that marks Jingoism.[3]

[1] *Man and Culture*, p. 339.   [2] Same, p. 174.
[3] John A. Hobson, *The Psychology of Jingoism*, Chapter I, London, 1900.

Both literacy and the Press are offspring of the machine age. The Press lives by advertising ; advertising follows circulation, and circulation depends on excitement. " What sells a newspaper ? " A former associate of Lord North-cliffe answers :

> The first answer is " war." War not only creates a supply of news but a demand for it. So deep-rooted is the fascination in war and all things appertaining to it that . . . a paper has only to be able to put up on its placard " A Great Battle " for its sales to mount up.[1]

This is the key to the proclivity of the Press to aggravate public anxiety in moments of crises.

So much for the general factors which condition the success of propaganda. Success depends upon traditional prejudices, objective connections between nations, and the changing level of popular irritability. No matter how skilful the propagandist may be in organizing his staff, selecting suggestions, and exploiting instruments of trans-mission, his manipulative skill will go for nought if there is no favourable juxtaposition of social forces to aid him.

The degree to which the propagandist is master of his fate depends in part upon the method of organization which he adopts. A number of agencies always engage in greater or less measure in war propaganda work ; the Foreign Office, the Diplomatic and Consular staffs ; the War Department, the General Staff and Field Headquarters ; and the principal service departments of internal administration. Since propaganda is, by its nature, incapable of complete segregation in the hands of one staff, unity must

---

[1] Kennedy Jones, *Fleet Street and Downing Street*, p. 108.

be achieved by the devious path of co-ordination, rather than by the simple act of exclusive delegation. During the last War the nations sought to minimize the dangers of contradiction, malproportion and duplication by resorting to one of three main types of co-ordination : the Press conference (Germany) ; the committee of executives, each responsible for a principal branch of propaganda work (Great Britain) ; and the single propaganda executive, operating in the name of the principal departments (the United States). The Germans got no further than common Press conferences and sporadic efforts at co-ordination because of the excessive friction between tneir civil and military authorities. Except for special commissioners who were sent to certain of the most important foreign countries, the French relied upon their existing agencies of government. The British were finally constrained to set up a committee of executives of approximately ministerial importance, each one of whom was charged with some such important branch of propaganda as enemy, home, allied or neutral. By securing a man of prestige to head each important service, policy was itself occasionally modified for the better. Northcliffe brought the Cabinet to straighten out its policy toward the Italians and the Jugo-Slavs, and the results vindicated the maxim that policy and propaganda should go hand in hand. The United States solved its problem by creating an ex-officio committee of the heads of principal departments (State, War and Navy) and one earnest and aggressive man who did the effectual work. Integration in Creel's hands was justifiable because of the comparative simplicity of America's propaganda both at home and abroad. The British had to deal with such a complex of foreign problems that extreme integration might have stifled ready adjustment.

The war experience seems to warrant the belief that the directors of each important propaganda service should be men whose prestige equals that of the policy determining officers, and that the staff should be selected from newspapermen—rather than proprietors—from popular writers, and from the members of the new propaganda profession.

The War abundantly demonstrated that the relation between the propaganda services and the legislature is a thorny problem. The executive arm of a democratic government may pervert a propaganda bureau to partisan, personal or class ends, and it may bind the legislature in advance, by stimulating public opinion, to favour its own policy. The executive may use the bureau to popularize an erroneous picture of the facts, and the legislature, conscious of all this, may assail the executive in unmeasured terms and undermine public confidence in its leaders. The best adjustment here does not depend upon statutes or ordinances, but upon the cultivation of informal channels of acquaintance and communication through which legislators may be brought into closer contact with the facts of the service. If matters go badly, they can, and should, protest. But their remarks should be grounded upon something more tangible than mere mistrust. It was the failure to close the gap between the legislator and the administrator, which led to the undignified and unjust criticism of the Committee of Public Information in the American Congress. There is no doubt, of course, that democratic governments must assume the task, regardless of all complicating difficulties, of mobilizing minds as well as men and money in war.

The general form of propaganda organization is a variable one, which the propagandist may adapt to his purposes. His problem, however, consists principally in selecting the social suggestions best calculated to evoke the desired responses.   In this he is governed, in the first instance, by the broad strategic aims of propaganda.   There are four major objectives :

(1) To mobilize hatred against the enemy ;
(2) To preserve the friendship of allies ;
(3) To preserve the friendship and, if possible, to procure the co-operation of neutrals ;
(4) To demoralize the enemy.

The general theory of the appeals to be employed to achieve each aim has been developed in the previous chapters of this inquiry, and may be summarized rather briefly at this point.

To mobilize the hatred of the people against the enemy, represent the opposing nation as a menacing, murderous aggressor. Represent the enemy as an obstacle to the realization of the cherished ideals and dreams of the nation as a whole, and of each constituent unit.   It is through the elaboration of war aims that the obstructive rôle of the enemy becomes particularly evident.   Represent opposing nation as satanic ;   it violates all the moral standards (*mores*) of the group, and insults its self-esteem.   The maintenance of hatred depends upon supplementing the direct representations of the menacing, obstructive, satanic enemy by assurances of ultimate victory.

To preserve friendly relations with an ally, the cardinal themes are our strenuous exertion in the prosecution of the war, and our hearty assent to the cherished war aims of the ally.   This may be supported by demonstrations of respect and esteem and by all the themes of domestic propaganda.

To win the friendship of a neutral, lead the neutral to identify his own interests with the defeat of our enemy.   In addition to the ordinary devices, seek to draw the neutral into active co-operation in some non-military capacity.   If all else fails, re-enforce pacifism, by portraying the horrors of war, and the unwillingness of the enemy to make peace, and stir up trouble between two neutrals.

To demoralize the enemy, substitute new hates for old. The edge of animosity may be somewhat blunted by direct counterstimulation,   but diversion depends mainly upon spreading discouragement and instigating defeatism.   The way is then paved for violent campaigns against allies, against the governing class, and among national minorities, against the unity of the state.

These themes were present in each war propaganda during the last War, but some of them were more effectively utilized by one belligerent than another.   The British were amazingly successful in the development of humanitarian war aims. The Germans aroused much resentment and suspicion abroad by talking about a war of German Kultur, and by underplaying the humanitarian ideal.   The British talked about a war to protect international law and to guarantee the sanctity of treaties, and they fought against a monster, known as autocratic militarism, in the name of democracy. British public men began to talk about a war to end war long before the German statesmen learned this vocabulary. Indeed, the colourless and halting pronouncements of Bethmann-Hollweg seemed more like concessions wrested from an unimaginative soul than programmes promulgated by a determined leader. Wilsonian phraseology touched the imagination of powerful elements throughout the world. In the duel of words the Germans fought with pasteboard against steel.

The Germans were never able to efface the initial impression that they were aggressors. This was due in part to the stupidity of their own appeals. They continued to talk about " Einkreisung " in America, where the danger of encirclement is a theoretical conjecture for which there is no counterpart in recent American tradition. They never dramatized the aggressiveness of their enemies as did the Allies, who invented the myth of the " Potsdam Council." They never succeeded in getting over the idea of a war hatched by a vain and dissolute uncle (Edward VII.) in a fit of pique at the success of his nephew (William II.) ; they failed to humanize and dramatize the diplomatic game, and held fast to diplomatic jargon and German catchwords, which lacked fire and fury in America.

Much of the German propaganda proved to be a boomerang. It is appalling that responsible directors of propaganda should have done everything in their power to circulate the charge that the Belgians were sniping. The Kaiser went so far as to make a public protest to President Wilson. The truth is that the report that the Belgians were sniping aroused admiration in America. It seemed to show how plucky these little Belgians really were, for the American public was a civilian public, and it knew that

Belgium was little and that Germany was big, and it cheered whenever the underdog bit.

The explanation of the maladroitness of the German propaganda is partly the influence which the military mind had upon it. To the soldier it is utterly inexcusable for a civilian to shoot a man in uniform. He has a strict code of ethics, which is dictated by consideration for his own skin, and he distinguishes sharply between what is permitted a man in uniform, and what is permitted a man out of uniform. These elementary distinctions are vague, and nearly meaningless to the public mind in such a country as the United States, where military training is the exception and not the rule. The American cartoonists reflected the civilian mind when they lampooned the big, coarse German, who howled to heaven that the little fellow whom he was beating had stung him with a pebble from a sling shot. The failure of the Germans to neutralize the Cavell incident has already been alluded to, and it typifies a military mind which is opaque to the civilian point of view.

Instead of complaining about the snipers in Belgium the Germans would have been better advised to have appointed a distinguished jury of neutrals to investigate the Welfare of the Belgian people, and to have broadcasted its report all over the world. As it was, they never neutralized the effect of the Bryce report.

The Germans cast no anchors to windward during the opening weeks of the War. They talked about the invincible German army, and predicted victory on a definite date.[1]

---

[1] The reason their propaganda began rather late and lost many openings was that they expected an early military victory.

They did not advertise the invasions in East Prussia, and their march through Belgium and northern France seemed to belie any theory of unpreparedness.

The French propaganda was lucid and simple. Her retiring armies told a *prima facie* story of who had been prepared for the War (after the early cloud of false news had blown aside), and her chief propaganda was that of simple satanism. The Germans were never able to popularize so striking an epithet as " Hun " or " Boche " and their clumsy exhortations to hate or their sneering references to the " Alllies," were much less powerful and invidious. The French vocabulary had powerful words like humanity and democracy, which reverberated with a tremendous clang abroad.

Little attention has been paid here to that aspect of influencing, which is often called " propaganda of the deed." By this is usually meant some isolated act of violence, which is intended to produce a powerful impression. The dropping of bombs upon enemy cities was less for immediate military and strategic purposes, than for propaganda purposes. It was supposed that civilian moral would crack under the strain of perpetual fear. This, besides the propaganda of frightfulness and other acts of frightfulness, was supposed to produce discouragement and defeatism.

Since much of the talk about frightfulness during the last War was sheer propaganda against the enemy, the effect of overt acts of this kind can be judged by the influence of such propaganda. On the whole, its chief result was to stiffen the determination of the people to defend themselves.

It may be unreliable, but there is a story with a flash of insight which tells about the German aviator who objected to dropping any more bombs on London, because he had not entered the War to be a recruiting officer for the British army. Civilians become habituated to raids, as Londoners did to the Zeppelin raids, and humour and ridicule soften the trial. The London stores advertised all sorts of accessories for " Zeppelin parties," and one is even supposed to have offered a special line of ' Zepp nighties."

The Allied propaganda of discouragement made little impression on the Germans until 1918. Indeed, the British wasted some of their early effort on vain boastings, when the German army was actually in victorious march against them. The American propaganda against the Germans was essentially a propaganda of discouragement and revolution. It was the British who did most of the propaganda of dissolution against Austro-Hungarian armies, and they scored notable successes. Success in propaganda of this kind depends much more upon the existence of strains and stresses in an enemy state than does success in propaganda among neutrals.

The preceding paragraphs have contrasted the strategy of some of the principal War propagandas, and rehearsed the general theory of how to select powerful appeals for the achievement of the four propaganda aims. There are humbler criteria of tactical nature, which the working propagandist applies to each suggestion. The tactical objectives may be summarized thus :

1. To arouse the interest of specific groups ;
2. To nullify inconvenient ideas ;
3. To avoid untruth which is likely to be contradicted before the achievement of the strategic purpose.

Effective propaganda is catholic in its appeal. It ignores no loyalty inside a nation. Protestants, Catholics, Jews, workers, financiers, farmers, merchants, city dwellers, and ruralites, sportsmen and philosophers, men of affairs and academicians, women and men, old and young ; every possible line of cleavage in the nation is appealed to by some direct or indirect device.[1]

R. J. R. S. Wreford exactly described this process when he said that the expert propagandist

> must decide as to the public which is most likely to be, or to become, sympathetically disposed toward the interests which he represents ; he must then select the aspects of those interests best calculated to appeal to the predilections of this public ; and he must then present these aspects in an attractive manner.[2]

Propaganda material must reach the meanest as well as the keenest intelligence. In the case of the crude prophecies of victory which were made during the War, it was safe to predict that they would carry reassurance to the most superstitious and credulous strata of the population, but that the sophisticated would pass them contemptuously by. It is perfectly safe to launch the crude and sophisticated together, for the people capable of reacting to the latter will not be estranged by the former ; they will merely remain indifferent and condescending. A cock-and-bull story about the Kaiser's lust for war, as revealed by his habit of spitting three times whenever the Union Jack was displayed, would

---

[1] For an example, see the description of Lithuanian propaganda on page 118.
[2] " Propaganda Good and Evil," 19th Century and After, 93 (1923) : 514–524. He patly defined propaganda as " the dissemination of interested fact and opinion."

probably not win Belgravia, no matter how popular it might be in Poplar. But a learned tome, prepared with all the dexterity of the trained academician, could defend the same general theme to the satisfaction of an intelligent public. Part of the superiority of British propaganda during the War was due to its amazing suppleness. In 1917 the journalist Arthur Bullard commented on this fact and wrote,

> The appeal which brought the first wave of volunteers was " Bleeding Belgium," the duty of the strong as good sportsmen to defend the weak. Then the attempt was made to stir national pride by posters quoting the Kaiser's alleged insulting reference to " the contemptible little English Army." An effort was made to frighten the people by the supposed danger of invasion. Somewhat later, pictures were displayed of the famous treaty which had been called a " scrap of paper." Every note was sounded from rage against " the baby killers " to fidelity to the pledged words as the basis of international relations. But by far the greatest response came on the appeal to demo-cratic idealism, the issue between popular rule and military despotism.[1]

Every suggestion must have an interesting appeal to a definite group, but some suggestions must be expressly designed to nullify inconvenient ideas. This brings us to the second tactical standard of good propaganda, which appears in the conduct of war influencing. When a government undertakes to influence the people within its own boundaries, it is usually able to control the cable, telegraph, telephone, Press, postal and wireless services, while war lasts. But psychological frontiers never coincide with geographical frontiers, and summary suppression is never a complete

---

[1] *Mobilizing America*, p. 44.

success. Governments learn to nullify rather than to conceal undesirable ideas.

Part of this technique is the control of emphasis.   Under-emphasis may be procured in the Press by relegating an item to an obscure column with an inconspicuous headline, by incorporating in another story, by omitting detail, by contradiction on the part of the writer or " witness," by quotations which cast doubt upon the assertion and related devices.   Conversely, favourable ideas may be given pro-minent columns, striking headlines, independent treatment, circumstantial detail, impressive corroboration and ceaseless repetition.

In practice, the simplest mode of nullifying important reports is by the device of compensation.   It is ridiculous to pretend that the enemy never wins a point.   The depressing news of an enemy gain should, however, be counterbalanced by a simultaneous gain.   This was what Winston Churchill used to do at the Admiralty, for

> he would hold on to a bit of bad news for a time on the chance of getting a bit of good news to publish as an offset, and I must say that it not infrequently came off.[1]

When American preparations began to assume disquieting proportions, the German Press played up the collapse of Russia.

Compensation sometimes takes the form of pointing out that the enemy is as badly off as the home public.   At one time during the War, the food administration in Berlin announced that 50 grammes of fresh lard would be distributed

---

[1] Brownrigg, *Indiscretions of a Naval Censor*, p. 13.

on a certain day, but circumstances intervened and it became impossible to make good. The disappointment of the people was somewhat appeased by the publication of impressive statistics of the huge losses of lard, to which the enemy had been subjected by the U-Boat campaign.

The most convenient mine of counter-propaganda material, is the opposition Press inside a foreign country. The German Press greeted the appointment of Foch to the supreme command by reprinting some articles in the French radical Press, which interpreted the appointment as a last straw, admitting that bad leadership had brought about the present plight at the front.

Unfavourable intelligence may be nullified by a flat denial, but defence by denial is not of itself efficacious when alarming news is abroad. Defence by admission and justification usually accomplishes more, especially when placed in the form of a counter-attack. Certain losses at the front may be covered by ostentatious hints at a great plan to draw the enemy from his base of supplies and snare him. Poison gas may be justified by assaulting the cruel, inhuman and illegal methods of warfare to which the enemy has resorted.

The public should be prepared in advance for the occurrence of an event, which might otherwise produce an undesirable repercussion. Thus precautions should be taken to discredit an authority which is to render an ultimate verdict, and which is almost certain to be unfriendly. The Germans looked with open contempt upon the panel selected to inquire into the Belgian atrocities, and they blackguarded both its integrity and its technique before publishing its results.

The public may have bad news " broken " to it gently by publishing a disquieting question, followed by a few facts, and then by the worst. Panic is thus circumvented, since the processes of discounting the future have produced a certain stability of response in the public mind.

When it is proposed to inaugurate a policy to which there may be some objection, it is possible to instigate a demand for the very policy which it is intended to introduce. This is the indirect initiative, or, as a Belgian student of propaganda[1] has christened it, the *initiative éventée* (the fanned initiative). He observed its operations at the time of the Brest Litovsk negotiations between Germany and Russia. There was a great deal of objection in Germany among the parties of the Left to a downright policy of annexation, so the Government proceeded cautiously. The *Kölnische Volks-zeitung* published a report that the English were negotiating with Russia for the right to occupy the Riga Islands. Instantly there were spontaneous editorials throughout Germany, demanding prompt action by the Imperial Government to forestall the accursed British. The Government took the islands.

Bad news and unwanted criticism may be nullified by distracting the attention of the public from them. A distraction is managed by springing a sensation which is unrelated to the inconvenient focal point of attention. The arrival of the *Deutschland* served this purpose in Germany at a dull moment during the War.

Yet a third general tactical standard has emerged in the course of our analysis. It is concerned with the relation of

---

[1] He occupies an official position at present.

propaganda to truth. To what extent is it necessary for the suggestions employed in propaganda to conform to the canons of critical veracity ?

Actual propaganda, wherever studied, has a large element of the fake in it. This varies from putting a false date line on a despatch, through the printing of unverified rumours, the printing of denials in order to convey an insinuation, to the " staging " of events. One of the world war fakes was the use of pictures of the Jewish pogrom of 1905, somewhat retouched, as fresh enemy atrocities. Of a similar type was the following : the London *Daily Mirror* of August 20th, 1915, published a picture of three German officers, who held various vessels in their hands. The sub-title was, " Three German Cavalrymen loaded with gold and silver loot," which they had taken in Poland. This was, in fact, a defaced reproduction of a picture, which had originally appeared in the *Berliner Lokalanzeiger* for the 9th of June, 1914, and which had shown the winners of the cavalry competition in the Grünewald. The officers had cups and trophies in their hands. The sub-title read :

> Vom Armee-Jagdrennen in Grünewald. Von links : Lt. Prieger, Zweiter : Lt. v. Egan-Krieger. Dritter : Lt., v. Herder. Sieger.[1]

Sir Campbell Stuart, looking back upon the British propaganda from the vantage ground of a victorious peace, has written that " only truthful statements " should be used in propaganda. This seems, in the light of practice, an impracticable maxim. It was not unusual during the War

---

[1] Ferdinand Avenarius exposed several of these falsifications during the War in the booklet, *Bild als Verleumder*, the enlarged, post-war edition of which is named *Die Mächte im Weltwahn*. A French rejoinder was named *L'imposture par l'image*.

to invent a great deal of material out of whole cloth. One of the best examples of this sort of thing was the famous cadaver story. Two captured photographs chanced to come to the desk of the Chief of the British Army Intelligence, Brigadier General J. V. Charters. One of them showed dead German soldiers being hauled away for burial behind the lines, and the other showed dead horses on the way to the soap factory. Knowing the reverence of the Chinese for their ancestors and the uncertainty of Chinese opinion toward the Germans, he thoughtfully interchanged the titles of the two pictures, and sent the edited material to Shanghai for release. " German cadavers on way to the soap factory," soon found its way to Europe and America and spread distaste and contempt of all things German.[1]

This was, of course, a plain lie. But it was plausible, and it was incapable of complete refutation during the War. During war, plenty of horrors are sure to occur. They grow dank and rank on every hand, and a mustard seed of truth may blossom and bloom. Indeed, a very sophisticated British soldier, a literary man, who was not one to be taken in by this sort of thing, related something in his own experience which might have given rise to a story of this kind. Shortly after having heard this tale for the first time, he was engaged in active fighting in Bellicourt. A British shell squashed a German field kitchen, and what he saw when he went to inspect the ruins, gave the clue to the " corpse factory."

[1] See the N.Y. *Times*, 20 October, 1925. Will Irwin, the able journalist who took the trouble to try to verify the atrocity tales of the War, has described several versions of the story that German soldiers cut off the hands of Belgian babies and carried them along as souvenirs. He found them all unproved and wildly improbable. Admiral Sims has categorically declared that the reports of the terrible inhumanity of submarine commanders was, with a single exception, pure fabrication.

A quite simple case. Shells had gone into cookhouses of ours, long before then, and had messed the cooks with the stew.[1]

The truth about the relation of truth to propaganda seems to be that it is never wise to use material which is likely to be contradicted by certain unconcealable events before the political objective of propaganda is attained. It is foolish to promise victory on a definite date in the imminent future, because the prediction may be falsified by the event and lead to a certain backwash of discouragement and suspicion. It is perfectly permissible to assert that ultimate success is sure, even though no critically-trained intelligence could accept such a statement as proved, because it is impossible to disprove this proposition before the attainment or the total eclipse of all hope of attaining the political objective.

It is evident that propaganda must avoid self-contradiction in the same context addressed to the same group or to groups in intimate contact with one another. There is comparatively little danger in telling the Protestants through their official organs that the war is a great Protestant crusade, and in encouraging the Catholics to regard it as a great Catholic movement ; but it would be absurd to mix the appeals to the same audience. Every special group tends to make the war over in its own image, and the task of the propagandist is usually to facilitate, rather than to fabricate.

The three tactical principles which have just been recapitulated, may be stated in these words :

1. Suggestions should be circulated which promise to arouse the interest of specific groups.

[1] C. E. Montague, *Disenchantment*, p. 93.

2. Suggestions should be chosen to nullify inconvenient ideas which cannot be suppressed.

3. Suggestions should be used which are likely to pass uncontradicted until the propaganda aim is realized, and this implies, in particular, that self-contradiction in the same context to the same public must be avoided.

The successful choice of propaganda material according to these standards presupposes accurate prediction, not only of the immediate results of its circulation, but of the counter-currents which may be instigated. If methods of prior testing can be devised, the propagandist will approximate somewhat closer to the omniscience once imputed to him by a New York newspaper, which wrote,

> the public mind to the trained propagandist is a pool into which phrases and thoughts are dropped like acids, with a foreknowledge of the reactions that will take place, just as Professor Loeb at the Rockefeller Institute can make a thousand crustaceans stop swimming aimlessly about in the bowl and rush with one headlong impulse to the side where the light comes from, merely by introducing into the water a little drop of a chemical.[1]

Thus far, our survey of the means of propaganda has covered the methods of organizing and the criteria for selecting suggestions for strategic or tactical reasons. There remains the problem of choosing from among the numerous instruments of transmission which are available. Suggestions may be spoken, written, pictorial[2] or musical, and

[1] New York *Tribune*, July 12th, 1918. Cited in Military Intelligence booklet on *Propaganda in its Military and Legal Aspects*, p. 93. Stern-Rubarth has named the " *Prüfung der möglicher Rückwirkung* " among his five principles. See his *Propaganda als politisches Instrument*.

[2] The literature of caricature, cartoon and illustration during the War is reviewed in L. M. Salmon, *The Newspaper and the Historian*. See especially p. 381 and after. Karl Demeter dealt with the film propaganda of the Entente in the *Archiv f. Politik u. Geschichte*, 4 (1925) : 214-231.

the possible variations in the form of the stimulus-carrier are infinite. The soundest method for the propagandist to follow is to cultivate the habit of identifying himself imaginatively with the subjects to be influenced, and to explore all the possible avenues of approach to their attention. Consider, from this point of view, a group of people who are riding in a street car. They may be influenced by placards posted inside the car, by posters on the billboards along the track, by newspapers which they read, by conversations which they overhear, by leaflets which are openly or surreptitiously slipped into their hands, by street demonstrations at halting places, and possibly by yet other carriers of suggestions.

Of possible occasions for suggestion there is no end. People walk along the streets or ride in automobiles, trams, subways, elevated trains, boats, electrical or steam railways ; people congregate in theatres, churches, lecture halls, eating places, athletic parks, concerts, barber shops and beauty parlours, coffee-houses and drug stores ; people work in offices, warehouses, mills, factories and conveyances. An inspection of the habit patterns of each community reveals a web of mobility routes and congregating centres, which may be taken advantage of for the dissemination of interested fact and opinion.

No *obiter dicta* about the comparative values of a given system of transmitting stimuli can have the same importance as the habit of mind which enables the propagandist to test each given situation for its inherent possibilities. The forms of suggestions are few and elemental, but the possible occasions and carriers are infinite. The technical literature on advertising is full of the most precise information on the effect of different colours, sizes, shapes and elevations of outdoor posters on suggestion. All this is indispensable to the working propagandist, but it is distinctly ancillary to the problem of achieving and preserving a perspective on the problem of control, which uses broad and rather flexible categories of analysis. These are the leading questions : What are the proposed subjects of stimulation doing ? How many separate occasions can be isolated ? How many spoken, written, pictorial, musical or demonstrative suggestions can be interposed ? What are carriers by which they may be transmitted into the experience-world of the subjects ?

For the sake of suggesting the more common instruments of propaganda, Mr. Creel's summary of the work of the Committee on Public Information may be quoted :[1]

Thirty odd booklets were printed in several languages. Seventy-five million copies were circulated in America, and many million copies were circulated abroad. Tours were arranged for the Blue Devils (French soldiers), Pershing's Veterans, and the Belgians, and mass meetings were arranged in many communities. Forty-five war conferences were held. The Four Minute Men commanded the volunteer services of 75,000 speakers, operating in 5,200 communities, and making a total of 755,190 speeches.

With the aid of a volunteer staff of several hundred translators, the Committee supplied the foreign language Press of America with selected articles. It planned war exhibits for the state fairs of the United States, a series of inter-Allied war expositions, and secured millions of dollars-worth of free advertising space from the Press, periodical, car and outdoor advertising forces of the country.

It used 1,438 drawings prepared by volunteers for the production of posters, window cards and similar material.

[1] Adapted from George Creel, *How We Advertised America.*

It issued a daily newspaper with a 100,000 circulation for official use. It ran an information service and syndicated feature articles for the Press. Plate-matter for the country Press, and specialized material for the labour, religious and women's Press was supplied. Moving pictures were commercially successful in America and effective abroad, such as " Pershing's Crusaders," " America's Answer," and " Under Four Flags."

Over two hundred thousand stereopticon slides were distributed. Still photographs were prepared, and a stream of 700 pictures per day of military activities were censored. Cable, telegraph and wireless were employed by an official news service. A special mail and photograph service was also built up for the foreign Press. Reading-rooms were opened abroad, schools and libraries were fitted out, photographs were displayed prominently.

Missions were sent to the important districts of the world to look after American propaganda on the spot.

The service cost the taxpayers $4,912,553, and earned $2,825,670·23 to be applied on expenses.

As we have seen, the problem of penetrating the enemy's country with propaganda material was solved during the last War by an ingenious device, the free balloon. After employing the Press of adjacent neutral countries, stationary balloons and aeroplanes, this mode of transmission was finally perfected and substituted. The Allies had the benefit of the prevailing westerly winds, and they laid down a barrage of print over the German lines.

One of the lessons to be drawn from the success of British propaganda in the United States is the cardinal importance of persons as means of carrying suggestion. No avenue of approach can safely be ignored, but the powers behind the impersonal agencies must be reached, and this is best managed by personal contact. The British were astute enough to work chiefly through Americans, and none of their agents came to the premature disgrace and humiliation that befell Dr. Dernburg.

This completes our brief summary of the conditions and methods of propaganda. Success, it may be reiterated, depends upon the astute use of propaganda means (organizations, suggestions, devices) under favourable conditions.

CHAPTER IX

THE RESULTS OF PROPAGANDA

AFTER this rapid review of the means and conditions of war propaganda we are in a position to undertake an appraisal of its results. The history of the late War shows that modern war must be fought on three fronts : the military front, the economic front, and the propaganda front. The economic blockade strangles, the propaganda confuses, and the armed force delivers the *coup de grace*. Employed in conjunction with the other arms of offence, propaganda saps the stamina of the armed and civilian forces of the enemy, and smoothes the path for the mailed fist of men and metal. The economic blockade slowly squeezes the vitality out of a nation, and depends for its maximum effect upon a prolonged struggle. Propaganda is likewise a passive and contributory weapon, whose chief function is to demolish the enemy's will to fight by intensifying depression, disillusionment and disagreement.

As the U.S. Military Intelligence described the function of propaganda, it

> attacks the whole army at its base ; threatens to cut it off from its base, to stop the flow of reinforcements, supplies, ammunition, equipment, food, comforts, and above all, to weaken the moral support that sustains the troops in the hardships and cruelties of war far from home.
>
> " Armies fight as the people think " was the wise epigram of the British General Applin. It might be extended to say that armies fight as armies think, for, as George William Curtis said : " Thoughts are Bullets."[1]

[1] *Propaganda in its Military and Legal Aspects*, Introduction.)

Notable successes in which propaganda had an important and perhaps a decisive part were scored in the last War.   In common with every other weapon of attack, propaganda has a surprise value, which the Central Powers realized to the full, in the ingenious propaganda offensive, which preceded their attack upon the Italians in 1917 at Caporetto. The spirit of the Italian armies was dissipated, and their lines cracked and broken.   In reply, the Allies won a striking success in 1918, when they forced the postponement of the Austro-Hungarian offensive against Italy, from April until June, by sowing demoralization among the troops of the subject nationalities.   Mutinous troops blew up ammunition dumps behind the lines, and sabotaged the whole military plan.

One of the gravest triumphs of the War was won when the Germans put the Russians out of the running.   They strained every muscle to complete the disintegration which culminated in the second Revolution.   They permitted the famous " sealed car " to convey Lenin and forty associates from Switzerland, across Germany on their way to Russia.   The ruthless Bolshevists accepted aid from any quarter and completed the job, in spite of all the frantic work of the American Red Cross and the special propaganda services of the Entente group.

But the crowning victory of the War was at the expense of the Germans.   German moral depended upon the hope that the victory which had been so many times within their grasp, was just over the horizon.   Strained to the breaking point by the inexorable clutch of the economic blockade, their great hopes of the spring and summer of 1918 crumpled into rubbish, the German army and the German people were ready to lend an ear to the seductive voice of Mr. Wilson.

If the great generalissimo on the military front was Foch, the great generalissimo on the propaganda front was Wilson. His monumental rhetoric, epitomizing the aspirations of all humanity in periods at once lucid and persuasive, was scattered far and wide over Germany. He declared war upon autocracies everywhere, and solemnly adhered to his distinction between the German people and the German rulers. His speeches were one prolonged instigation to revolt. He and Lenin were the champion revolutionists of the age. Throughout the entire War his pronouncements had won a substantial measure of confidence and respect in the minds of that minority of democratically-minded men, who longed to transform the pre-war Germany of class discrimination and special privilege. And when the clouds of adversity darkened the sky in 1918, they were joined by immense numbers of their compatriots, pinched by privation and despair, anxiously searching the heavens for portents of a soft peace. They turned, not to Clemenceau—hard, relentless vulture, poised like an avenging conscience, to tear at the vitals of a fallen adversary, nor to Lloyd George —nimble, unstable and uncertain, but to this mysterious figure in the White House, aloof from the ordinary passions of petty men, who spoke in elegiac prose of a better world, when wars should be no more and a brotherhood of democratic peoples should bury their heritage of ancestral rancour, and march toward a world of fellowship and reconciliation. It was to this man, mercilessly ridiculed and caricatured from one end of Germany to another through long years of hesitation and then of belligerency, that the Germans turned in their extremity.

Could it be that at last a statesman had arisen to lead the peoples of the world in the path of friendship and peace ? Had a great prophet at last soared above vindictiveness and animosity to bring understanding to a harassed universe ? This butt of ribald jest was transformed at a stroke in those closing months of hunger, insecurity, foreboding and hallucination into a saviour. The people grasped at straws and saw deliverers where they had seen but pedantic fools before.

Such matchless skill as Wilson showed in propaganda has never been equalled in the world's history. He spoke to the heart of the people as no statesman has ever done. For a few brief months he embodied the faith of the idealists in a better world, and the last desperate hope of the defeated peoples for a soft peace. He was raised to a matchless pinnacle of prestige and power, and his name was spoken with reverence in varied accents in the remotest corners of the earth.

Just how much of Wilsonism was rhetorical exhibitionism and how much was the sound fruit of sober reflection will be in debate until the World War is a feeble memory. From a propaganda point of view it was a matchless performance, for Wilson brewed the subtle poison, which industrious men injected into the veins of a staggering people, until the smashing powers of the Allied armies knocked them into submission. While he fomented discord abroad, Wilson fostered unity at home. A nation of one hundred million people, sprung from many alien and antagonistic stocks, was welded into a fighting whole, " to make the world safe for democracy." And the magic of his eloquence soothed the suspicions which Central and South America cherished toward the mighty colossus of the North, and brought most of them into the War on the Allied side.

The propaganda of disintegration which was directed against the tottering realm of the Hapsburgs bore fruit in disaffection and ultimate secession among the Czechs, Slovaks, Rumanians, Croats, Poles and Italians. The Balfour Declaration hastened the reversal of Jewish sympathies in 1917.

Some of the triumphs of propaganda were in the field of recruiting. In the race for Allies, the Germans won in Bulgaria and Turkey, but the honours went to the Allies in the United States, Italy, Rumania, Greece and in a wide array of lesser countries, and Germany stood isolated in sympathy, except for Spain and Sweden. The hand of the whole world was raised against the Teuton. The great tug of war in America was only won by the British and the French after a desperate struggle against the German propaganda. The French were admirable in the very simplicity of their appeal. They invoked the sacred name of Lafayette, implored the gods of democracy, blackguarded the Germans and advertised the Americans who had enlisted on the side of the French. The British had less traditional affection to draw upon, and much more to explain away, but they had the powerful asset of the cables and the good sense to work, not secretly, but just outside the glare of publicity. And neither the British nor the French were severely handicapped by a military-diplomatic programme, which hurled all their fine pretensions in their teeth.[1]

Now a formidable list could be drawn up of the propaganda drives which failed or which accomplished their objective after a long period of waiting. Not all the propagandas to instigate defeat, Revolution, or secession and to preserve friendship succeeded. After all, India, Egypt, Ireland and Morocco did not respond to the proddings of German agents to rise up as one man to cast off the yoke of the Englishman and the Frenchman ; Austria-Hungary, Germany, Bulgaria and Turkey did hold out for four long years. France, Great Britain, and most of the Allies persisted through all discouragement to victory, in spite of the dangerous German peace offensive of 1916–17. But before regarding these negative results as a defeat for propaganda, it must be remembered that propaganda was not only an offensive weapon ; it was a powerful means of defence as well. Unity could be preserved just as it could be demolished by propaganda. Indeed, propaganda was present on both sides of every hotly-contested sector, and though it is one of those weapons whose precise effect is largely a matter of surmise, it is one which it would be foolhardy to neglect.

A defeated country naturally exaggerates the influence of propaganda. The Italians sought to save their faces after the Caporetto disaster[2] by complaining of the terrible and

[1] The importance of propaganda in neutral countries has been illustrated, of course, in many other wars before the last one. President Lincoln tried every expedient to stimulate the pro-North sentiment in England's industrial wage earners during the Civil War. He sent Henry Ward Beecher and perhaps a hundred other agents to England to plead the cause of the anti-slavery side. One of the most effective and original stunts was to send a ship loaded with foodstuffs, to relieve the suffering in the cities.

[2] The report of the special commission of inquiry into the Caporetto disaster which was appointed by the Italian Government is not now available, and complete judgment cannot be made upon the whole affair.

insidious German propaganda, and Ludendorff devotes a great many pages to explaining just how it was that he did not lose the War, and how the Alien and Radical riff-raff in the population collapsed behind the lines, leaving a sort of vacuum, in which the German troops fell, victorious to the end.

It is especially difficult to extricate the strands of propaganda influence from the means of control which are closely allied to it. When the Nivelle offensive drowned in a sea of blood in 1917, no less than twelve army corps were tainted by mutinous demonstrations. Soldiers began to start home, infuriated by the insensate butchery of their comrades. It was the remarkable work of General Pétain which restored orderly enthusiasm to the front and thwarted the ominous diversion of hatred which threatened to turn the French soldiery against their own leaders and away from the enemy. He relied by no means exclusively upon propaganda.[1]

But when all allowances have been made, and all extravagant estimates pared to the bone, the fact remains that propaganda is one of the most powerful instrumentalities in the modern world.[2] It has arisen to its present eminence in response to a complex of changed circumstances which have altered the nature of society. Small, primitive tribes can weld their heterogeneous members into a fighting whole

---

[1] For a description of his methods, see Mayer, *La psychologie du commandement*, and, in general, the reference in the section upon moral and military psychology in the bibliography.

[2] Sir Thomas More foreshadows the extensive use of propaganda in Utopia. He records how the Utopians spread distrust among their enemies by offering a reward for the capture or the voluntary surrender of prominent enemy leaders, and how they seek to divide the enemy by fostering the ambition of a rival to the reigning prince.

by the beat of the tom-tom and the tempestuous rhythm of the dance. It is in orgies of physical exuberance that young men are brought to the boiling point of war, and that old and young, men and women, are caught in the suction of tribal purpose.

In the Great Society it is no longer possible to fuse the waywardness of individuals in the furnace of the war dance ; a new and subtler instrument must weld thousands and even millions of human beings into one amalgamated mass of hate and will and hope. A new flame must burn out the canker of dissent and temper the steel of bellicose enthusiasm. The name of this new hammer and anvil of social solidarity is propaganda. Talk must take the place of drill ; print must supplant the dance. War dances live in literature and at the fringes of the modern earth ; war propaganda breathes and fumes in the capitals and provinces of the world

Propaganda is a concession to the rationality of the modern world. A literate world, a reading world, a schooled world prefers to thrive on argument and news. It is sophisticated to the extent of using print ; and he that takes to print shall live or perish by the Press. All the apparatus of diffused erudition popularizes the symbols and forms of pseudo-rational appeal ; the wolf of propaganda does not hesitate to masquerade in the sheepskin. All the voluble men of the day—writers, reporters, editors, preachers, lecturers, teachers, politicians—are drawn into the service of propaganda to amplify a master voice. All is conducted with the decorum and the trappery of intelligence, for this is a rational epoch, and demands its raw meat cooked and garnished by adroit and skilful chefs.

Propaganda is a concession to the wilfulness of the age. The bonds of personal loyalty and affection which bound a man to his chief have long since dissolved. Monarchy and class privilege have gone the way of all flesh, and the idolatry of the individual passes for the official religion of democracy. It is an atomized world, in which individual whims have wider play than ever before, and it requires more strenuous exertions to co-ordinate and unify than formerly. The new antidote to wilfulness is propaganda. If the mass will be free of chains of iron, it must accept its chains of silver. If it will not love, honour and obey, it must not expect to escape seduction.

Propaganda is a reflex to the immensity, the rationality and wilfulness of the modern world. It is the new dynamic of society, for power is subdivided and diffused, and more can be won by illusion than by coercion. It has all the prestige of the new and provokes all the animosity of the baffled. To illuminate the mechanisms of propaganda is to reveal the secret springs of social action, and to expose to the most searching criticism our prevailing dogmas of sovereignty, of democracy, of honesty, and of the sanctity of individual opinion. The study of propaganda will bring into the open much that is obscure, until, indeed, it may no longer be possible for an Anatole France to observe with truth that " Democracy (and, indeed, all society) is run by an unseen engineer."

NOTE ON BIBLIOGRAPHY

It is scarcely profitable in a study of this kind to rehearse the long list of printed materials which have been cited. Instead, a list that bears upon some of the main features of the general problem will be appended.

I. The Technique of Influencing International Attitudes, During and Since the War.

Angoff, Charles, " The Higher Learning goes to War," *American Mercury*, June, 1927, XI : 177–191.
Baudrillart, Mgr. Alfred, *Notre Propaganda*, Paris, 1916.
„   „   „   *Une campagne française*, Paris, 1917.
Baschwitz, Kurt, *Der Massenwahn*, München, 1924.
Bernstorff, Count, *My Three Years in America*, New York, 1920.
Blankenhorn, Heber, *Adventures in Propaganda*, Boston, 1919.
Brownrigg, Rear-Admiral Sir Douglas, *Indiscretions of the Naval Censor*, London, 1920.
Busch, Moritz, *Bismarck*, New York, 1898.
" Cincinnatus," *Der Krieg der Worte.* Stuttgart, Berlin, 1916.
Cook, Sir Edward Tyas, *The Press in War-time, with some account of the Official Press Bureau.* London, 1920.
Creel, George, *How We Advertised America*, New York, 1920.
Démartial, Georges, *La guerre de 1914. Comment on mobilisa les consciences.* Paris, 1922.
Demeter, Karl, " Die Filmspropaganda der Entente im Weltkriege," *Archiv f. Politik und Geschichte*, 4 (1925) : 214–231.
Drouilly, J. Germain et Guérinon, E., *Les chefs-d'œuvre de la propagande allemande.* Nancy, Paris, Strasbourg, 1919.
Got, A., " La littérature pangermaniste d'après-guerre," *Mercure de France*, 167 ; 403–21, October 15th, 1923.
Graux, Dr. L., *Les fausses nouvelles de la grande guerre.* Paris, 1919. 5 tomes.
Hallays, André, *L'opinion allemande pendant la guerre*, 1914–18, Paris, 1919.
Haas, Albert, *Die Propaganda im Ausland.* Weimar, 1916.

Hansi (Johann Jacob Waitz) et E. Tonnelet, *À travers les lignes ennemies. Trois années d'offensive contre le moral allemand.* Paris, 1922.

Hartmann, Peter, *Französische Kulturarbeit am Rhein.* Leipzig, 1921.

Kerkhof, Karl, *Der Krieg gegen die deutsche Wissenschaft.* Charlottenburg, 1922.

Lasswell, Harold D., " The Status of Research on International Propaganda and Opinion," *Proceedings of the American Sociological Society.* Chicago, 1926.

Ludendorff, General, *Meine Erinnerungen.* Berlin, 1919.

Marchand, Louis, *L'offensive morale des Allemands en France pendant la guerre.* Paris, 1920.

Melville, Lewis, " German Propaganda Societies," *Quarterly Review,* 230 (1918) : 70–88.

Merriam, Charles E., " American Publicity in Italy," *American Political Science Review.* November, 1919.

Military Intelligence Branch, Executive Division, General Staff, U.S.A., *Propaganda in its Military and Legal Aspects.* Washington, 1919,

Mühsam, Kurt, *Wie wir belogen wurden. Die amtliche Irreführung im Weltkrieg.* Berlin, 1920.

Parker, Sir Gilbert, " The United States and the War," *Harper's Magazine,* 136 (1918) : 521–531.

Prezzolini, Guiseppe, *Dopo Caporetto,* Roma, 1919.

Rivaud, A., " La propagande allemande," *Revue des sciences politiques,* July-September, 1922.

Rühlmann, Paul M., *Kulturpropaganda.* Charlottenburg, 1919.

Schönemann, F., *Die Kunst der Massenbeeinflussung in den Vereinigten Staaten von Amerika.* Stuttgart, 1924.

Steed, Henry Wickham, *Through Thirty Years.* New York, 1924. 2 vols.

Street, Major C. J. C., " Propaganda Behind the Lines," *Cornhill Magazine,* 3d. Series, 47 (1919) : 488–499.

Stuart, Campbell, *Secrets of Crewe House. The Story of a Famous Campaign.* London, 1920.

Stuelpnagal, Otto v., *Die Nachkriegs-Propaganda der Alliierten gegen Deutschland.* Berlin, 1922.

Whitehouse, Vira B., *A Year as a Government Agent.* New York, 1920.

Wiehler, *Deutsche Wirtschaftspropaganda im Weltkrieg.* Berlin, 1922.

Daily Extracts from the Foreign Press (June, 1915—).

Daily Digest of the Foreign Press (March 20th, 1916—).

Daily Review of the Foreign Press (March 23rd, 1916—).

Brewing and Liquor Interests and German (and Bolshevist) Propaganda. Hearings before a sub-committee on the Judiciary of the U.S. Senate, 65th Congress, 2nd Sess., Washington, 191. 3 vols.

The National German-American Alliance. Hearings before a sub-committee of the committee on the Judiciary. U.S. Senate, 65th Congress, 2nd Sess., Washington, 1918.

II. GENERAL STUDIES OF PUBLIC OPINION AND PROPAGANDA.

Adler, Georg, *Die Bedeutung der Illusionen für Politik und soziales Leben,* Jena, 1904.

Allport, F. H., and Hartman, D. A., " The Measurement and Motivation of a typical Opinion in a Certain Group," *American Political Science Review,* XIX, No. 4, November, 1925, 735–760.

Angell, Norman (Lane), *The Public Mind,* New York, 1927.

Bauer, Wilhelm, *Die öffentliche Meinung und ihre geschichtlichen Grundlagen.* Tübingen, 1914.

Bernays, E. L., *Crystallizing Public Opinion.* New York, 1923.

Birnbaum, Alfred, *Das Wesen der Propaganda. Eine Psychol. Studie,* Berlin, 1920.

Bogardus, E. S., " Analysing Changes in Public Opinion," *Journal of Applied Sociology,* IX, 5, May-June, 1925, 372–381 ; also *Proceedings of the American Sociological Society,* 1926.

Chassieriaud, R., *La formation de l'opinion publique.* Paris, 1914.

Christensen, A., *Politics and Crowd-Morality,* New York, 1915.

Conway, M., *The Crowd in Peace and War.* New York, 1915.

Deherme, Georges, *Les forces à régler. Le nombre et l'opinion publique.* Paris, 1919.

Dodge, R., " Psychology of Propaganda," *Religious Education,* 15 : 241–52, October, 1920.

Eltzbacher, *Die Presse als Werkzeug der auswärtigen Politik.* Jena, 1918.

Fluegge, G., " Zur Psychologie der Massen," *Preuss. Jahrb.*, 1921, 183, 345–369.

Gersdorf, Karl v., *Ueber den Begriff und das Wesen der öffentichen Meinung.* 1846.

Griffith, C. R., " A Comment upon the Psychology of the Audience," *Psychol. Monog.*, 1921, 30 (No. 136), 36–47.

Hayes, E. C., " The Formation of Public Opinion," *Journal of Applied Sociology*, 10 ; 6–9, September, 1925.

Hendrich, Franz Josias von, *Ueber den Geist des Zeitalters und die Gewalt der öffentlichen Meinung*, 1797.

Higham, C. F., *Looking Forward. Mass Education through Publicity.* London, 1920.

Holtzendorff, Franz v., *Wesen und Wert der öffentlichen Meinung.* München, 1880.

King, Clyde L., " Public Opinion as viewed by Eminent Political Theorists," *U. of Pennsylvania Public Lectures*, Philadelphia, 1916.

Kracauer, S., " Die Gruppe als Ideenträger," *Archiv f. Sozialw·* 49 (1922) : 594–622.

Kraus, Herbert, " Prolegomena zum Begriff der öffentlichen Meinung," *Festschrift.* Franz von Liszt, Berlin, 1911, 148–167.

Kulke, Eduard, *Zur Entwicklungsgeschichte der Meinungen*, Leipzig, 1891.

Kydd, Samuel, *A Sketch of the Growth of Public Opinion*, London, 1888.

Le Bon, *The Crowd* (12th edition). London, 1920.

————— *Les opinions et les croyances*, Paris, 1911.

Lee, Ivy L., *Publicity*, New York, 1925.

Lippmann, W., *Public Opinion.* New York, 1922.

„   „   *The Phantom Public.* New York, 1925.

Lipsky, Abram, *Man the Puppet.* New York, 1925.

Long, John C., *Public Relations*, New York, 1924.

Lowell, A. L., *Public Opinion in War and Peace.* Cambridge, 1923.

Lumley, F. E., " Propaganda," Chapter VIII, in *Means of Social Control.* New York, 1925.

Mackinnon, W. A., *History of Civilization and Public Opinion*, third edition, 2 vols., London, 1849.

(Mackinnon, W. A.), *On the Rise, Progress and Present State of Public Opinion in Great Britain and other parts of the World*, London, 1828.

Martin, E. D., *The Behavior of Crowds*, New York, 1920.

Millioud, M., " La propagation des idées," *Revue Philosophique*, 69 ; 580–600 ; 70 : 168–191.

Moysset, Henri, *L'opinion publique.* Lyon, 1910.

Papon, Jean Pierre, *De l'action de l'opinion sur le gouvernement*, 1788.

Park, R. E., *Masse und Publikum*, Bern, 1904.

Pieper, Karl, *Die Propaganda. Ihre Entstehung u. religiöse Bedeutung*, Aachen, 1922.

Plenge, Johann, *Deutsche Propaganda, Die Lehre von d. Propaganda als prakt. Gesellschaft. Mit e. Nachw. von Ludwig Raselius.* Bremen, 1922.

Quiett, G. C., and Casey, R., *Principles of Publicity*, New York, 1926.

Riis, R. W., and Bonner, C. W., *Publicity*, New York, 1926.

Ross, E. A., *Social Control*, New York, 1901.

Rossi, P., *Le suggesteur et la foule, psychologie du meneur*, Paris 1904.

Sagaret, J., " L'opinion," *Révue Philosophique*, LXXXVI (1918) : 19–38.

Salmon, L. M., *The Newspaper and Authority.* New York, 1923. *Newspaper and the Historian.* New York, 1923.

Schultze-Pfaelzer, Gerhard, *Propaganda, Agitation, Reklame. Eine Theorie des gesammten Werbewesens.* Berlin, 1923.

Schwertfeger, Bernhard, " Propaganda," *Handbuch der Politik*, V (1922) : 470–474.

Shepherd, W. J., " Public Opinion," *American Journal of Sociology*, XV (1909), 32–60.

Sighele, S., *Psychologie des Auflaufs und der Massenverbrechen*, Leipzig, 1897.

Stern-Rubarth, Edgar, *Die Propaganda als politisches Instrument.* Berlin, 1921.

Strong, E. K., " Control of Propaganda as a Psychological Problem," *Scientific Monthly*, 14 : 234–252, March, 1922.

Szirtes, Artur, *Zur Psychologie der öffentlichen Meinung.* Wien and Leipzig, 1921.

Tarde, G., *L'opinion et la foule*, Paris, 1901.

Thiébault, Dieudonné, *Traité sur l'esprit public*, Paris, An VI.

Thurstone, L. L., " The Method of Paired Comparisons for Social Values," *Journal of Abnormal and Social Psychology*, XXI, 4, January-March, 1927. (First of a series of papers dealing with the technique of measuring opinions.)

Tönnies, F., *Kritik der öffentlichen Meinung*. Berlin, 1922.

Wallas, Graham, *Human Nature and Politics*. London, 1908.

„   „   *The Great Society*. New York, 1914.

Weeks, A. D., *Control of the Social Mind*. New York. 1923.

Wilder, R. H., and Buell, K. L., *Publicity*. New York, 1923.

III. SPECIAL HISTORICAL STUDIES OF OPINION IN INTERNATIONAL POLITICS.

Alzona, Encarnacion, *French Contemporary Opinion of the Russian Revolution of* 1905. Col. U. Studies, No. 228, Vol. C, 1921.

Angell, Norman (Ralph Lane), *Patriotism under Three Flags*. London, 1903.

Ebbinghaus, Therese, *Napoleon, England und die Presse* (1800–1803), München u. Berlin, 1914.

Gazley, John G., *American Opinion of German Unification*, 1848–1871. Col. U. Studies, No. 267, Vol. CXXI, New York, 1926.

Martin, B. Kingsley, *The Triumph of Lord Palmerston*. London, 1924.

Périvier, A., *Napoléon journaliste*, Paris, 1918.

Price, Maurice T., *Christian Missions and Oriental Civilization*, Shanghai, 1924.

Raymond, Dora N., *Contemporary British Opinion during the Franco-Prussian War*. Col. U. Studies, No. 227, Vol. C, 1921.

Thompson, Geo. Carslake, *Public Opinion and Lord Beaconsfield*, 1875–1880, two vols., London, 1886.

IV. MORAL AND MILITARY PSYCHOLOGY.

Andrews, L. C., *Leadership, Military Training*. Philadelphia 1918.

„   „   *Military Manpower*. New York, 1920.

Campeano, M., *Essai de psychologie militaire individuelle et collective*. Paris, 1902.

Gallishaw, J., and W. Lynch, *The Man in the Ranks*. New York, 1917.

Gavet, André, *L'Art de commander*. Nancy, 1921.

Goddard, H. C., *Morale*. New York, 1918.

Gulick, L. H., *Morals and Morale*. New York, 1919.

Hall, G. S., *Morale*. New York, 1920.

Hocking, W. E., *Morale and its Enemies*. New Haven, 1918.

House, F. N., *Industrial Morale*. Chicago, 1924 (Thesis).

Mayer, Lieut., *La psychologie du commandement*. Paris, 1923.

Maxwell, W. N., *A Psychological Retrospect of the Great War*. New York, 1923.

Miller, A. H., *Leadership*. New York, 1920.

Munson, E. L., *The Management of Men*. New York, 1921.

Peterson, J., *Psychology of Handling Men in the Army*. Minneapolis, 1919.

Rohan, Henri, duc de, *Le parfait capitaine*. Paris, 1744.

Terman, L. M., " Psychology and Pedagogy of Leadership," *Pedagogical Review*, XI : 113–51.

Ziehen, A., *Die Psychologie grosser Heerführer*. Leipzig, 1916.

INDEX

231